∕MUST SEE
MILITARY HISTORY
TRAVEL GUIDES

CENTRAL LONDON TOP 50

Also from **MUST SEE**
MILITARY HISTORY

Must See Military History Travel Guides: USA Top 100 East of the Mississippi

MUST SEE
MILITARY HISTORY
TRAVEL GUIDES

CENTRAL LONDON TOP 50

Ron Varga

PUBLISHER

Must See Military History
PO Box 342
Valhalla NY 10595

ACKNOWLEDGEMENTS

Map data © OpenStreetMap contributors.

PUBLISHER'S CATALOGING-IN-PUBLICATION DATA

Names: Varga, Ron S., editor
Title: Must see military history travel guides: central London top 50 / Ron Varga
Description: Trade paperback first edition. | Valhalla, New York : Must See Military History, 2016. | Includes index.
Identifiers: LCCN 2016901938 | ISBN 978-0692632406
Subjects: LCSH: Military museums-Great Britain. | Museums-Great Britain. | BISAC: HISTORY / Europe / Great Britain. | TRAVEL / Special Interest / Military.
Classification: LCC: U13.A1 | DDC: 355.0074

Library of Congress Control Number: 2016901938

To our ancestors
who fought to build and protect our nation and civilization, and
to my family for passing on to me a love of their achievements.

To my wife and children
for their company on hundreds of visits to battlefields,
ceremonies, fortifications and museums over the decades.

CONTENTS

KEY

LOCATIONS

Maps

 Ceremony
Fortification
Aircraft
Warship
Museum
Naval museum

Visitor Info sections

Times ⟶ Abbreviations:
Costs
Facilities
Notes

- ★ Days as *Su*, *Mo*, *Tu*, ...
- ★ Weekend as *w/e*
- ★ Months as ***Jan***, ***Feb***, ...

APPENDIX: TIMELINES

Select Battles (Central and Greater London)	
54 BC	Caesar fought across the river at Westminster or Lambeth (or at Brentford eight miles west).
1066	After their defeat at Hastings, Saxons temporarily thwart the Normans at London Bridge.
1450	Jack Cade and rebels defeat a royal contingent at Sevenoaks before entering London.
1471	Yorkists defeat Lancastrians at Barnet in Wars of the Roses. Edward IV is crowned king.
1497	After a skirmish at Guildford, Henry VII defeats Cornish rebels at Deptford Bridge.
1642	Royalists defeat Parliament at Brentford but retreat the next day after London troops arrive.

Select Fortifications (Greater London PAGE 94 ONLY)	
500 BC	Loughton Camp is a 10-acre Iron Age hill fort in Epping Forest near town of Loughton.
450 BC	Caesar's Camp is a small Iron Age hill fort on Wimbledon Common. Little of it remains.
1070	Once a Saxon manor, it was taken by Normans, fortified, and made into Eltham Palace.
1088	Eynsford Castle is an early Norman "enclosure" castle. It was abandoned in 1312.
1937	Admiralty Chart Depot was fortified as a bunker for Navy staff as war approached.
1953	Kelvedon Hatch was a operational nuclear bunker until it was decommissioned in 1992.

INTRODUCTION

Dear Reader,

Welcome to the military history travel guide to central London.

London has a wealth of military history unrivalled by any other city. But how did a few square miles of woodland next to a marshy river at the edge of the world 2,000 years ago come to have the greatest martial heritage today?

London was founded at England's commercial crossroads soon after the Roman invasion of AD 43. As a successful ancient, then medieval, hub of trade, industry and population, London controlled trade routes and provided money, men, and equipment for armies and navies. Fortified to protect these assets, it was targetted and often fought over as were its northwest European peers. The city and its peers were also washed over by the common tides of history: Roman Empire, Germanic invaders, Viking invaders, feudal knights and castles, fire-arms and centralising state power, professional navies and armies, transoceanic empires and conflicts, French Revolutionary and Napoleonic Wars, and World Wars of the 20th century.

But London was even more importantly a center of regional government: provincial capital of the Roman Empire (c.61-410), administrative center of the Anglo-Scandinavian Empire (1016-1035), and the national capital of the Anglo-French Empire (1066-1558). However it was as imperial capital of the British Empire (1607-1997) that the city acquired historic arms and armour wherever the Empire wielded power, namely, everywhere. While London, in this way, was paralleled by capitals of other empires based in the region, it exceeded them in its wealth of military history just as the British Empire eclipsed the others to control a quarter of the earth's land mass and to dominate the seas.

This book showcases London's military treasures with 50 entries on the city's best events, locations and collections. Entries are grouped into chapters on Ceremonies, Fortifications, and Museums. Three museum chapters are subtitled: Aircraft & Ships (museums with aerospace/naval hardware), General & Sacred (non-military museums and churches with key contributions to the city's martial heritage), and Military & Naval (museums with an inherently military focus).

For each of the locations, this book provides details on its history (what happened there), description (what you can find there now), and useful visitor information (when is it open, how much does it cost, what facilities are available, and other noteworthy facts). We recommend you use contact information provided for each site to check times and dates prior to travelling.

If you have suggestions for sites you consider should be in the Top 50, or if you disagree with information presented in this book, we would like to hear from you at msmh.co. All suggestions will be considered for future editions, and corrections will be listed on our website. Until then, we hope you enjoy *Must See Military History Travel Guides: Central London Top 50*.

Ron Varga
Editor, Must See Military History

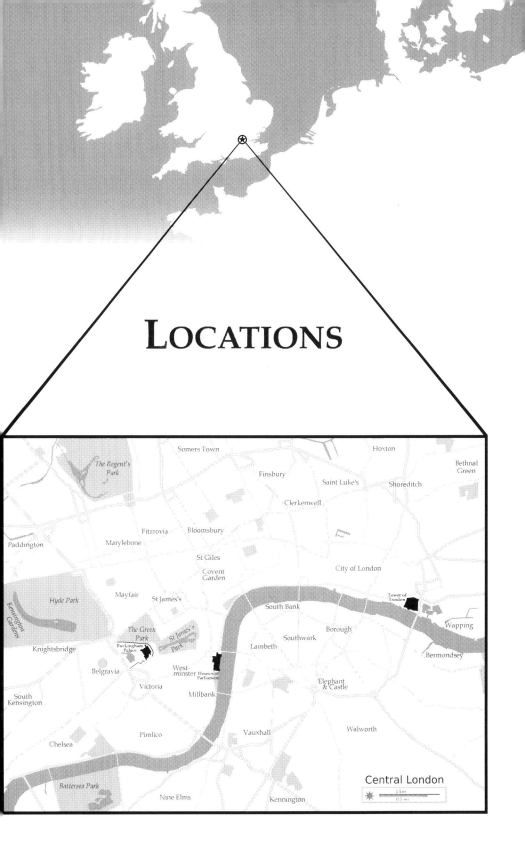

LOCATIONS

Central London

1 km
0.5 mi

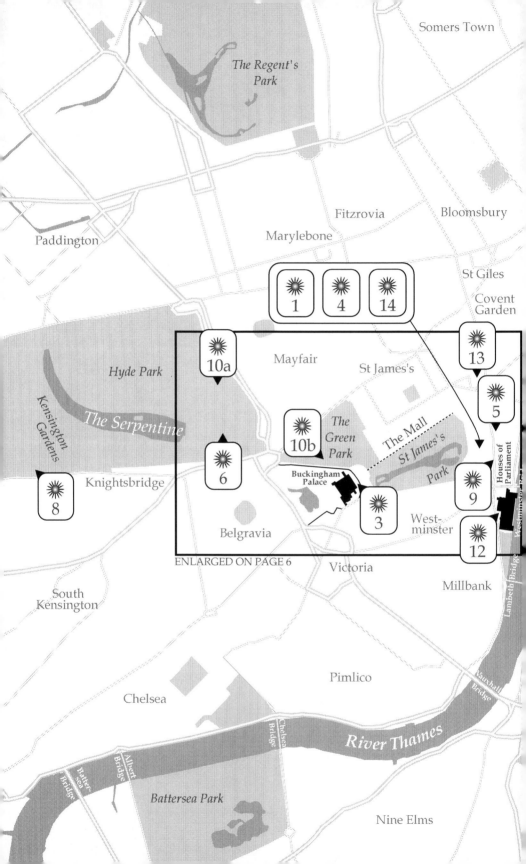

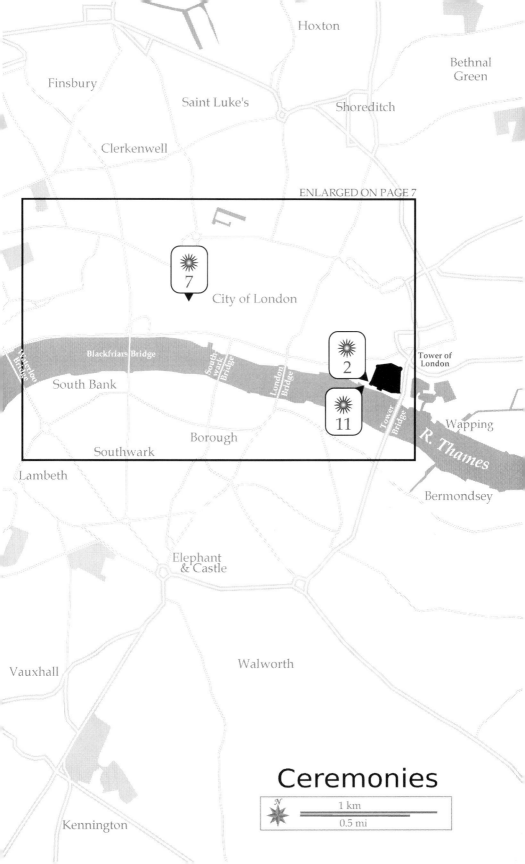

ENLARGED ON PAGE 7

Hoxton

Bethnal
Green

Finsbury

Saint Luke's

Shoreditch

Clerkenwell

☀
7

City of London

☀
2

Tower of
London

Blackfriars Bridge

Waterloo Bridge

South Bank

Southwark Bridge

London Bridge

☀
11

Tower Bridge

Wapping

R. Thames

Borough

Southwark

Bermondsey

Lambeth

Elephant
& Castle

Walworth

Vauxhall

Kennington

Ceremonies

N
1 km
0.5 mi

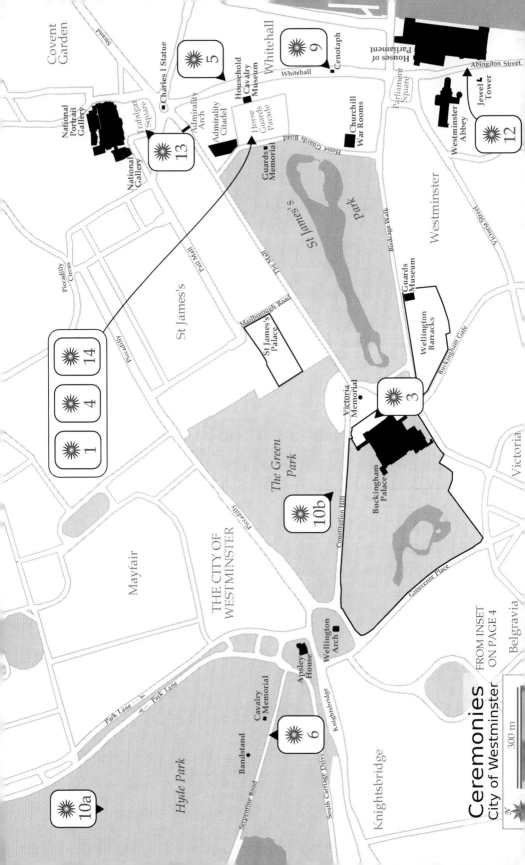

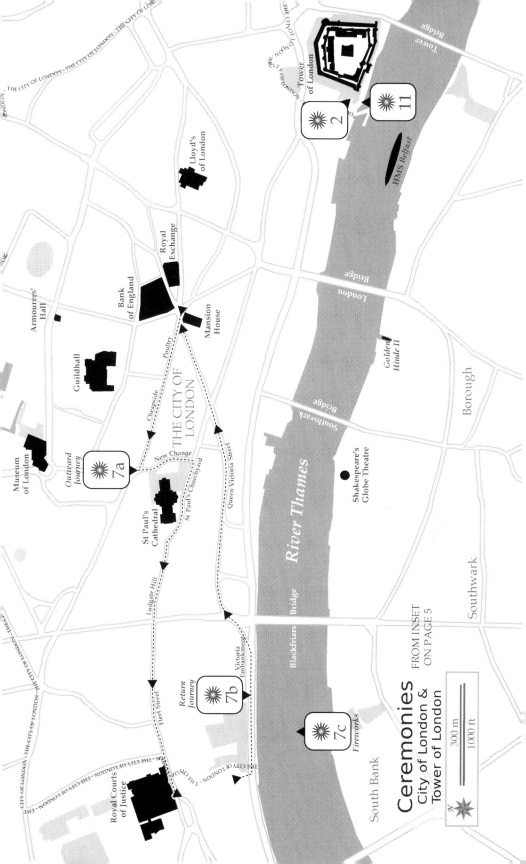

Ceremonies
City of London &
Tower of London

FROM INSET
ON PAGE 5

300 m
1000 ft

THE CITY OF LONDON · THE CITY OF LONDON · THE CITY OF LON

Tower Bridge

Tower of London

HMS Belfast

☀ 2   ☀ 11

Lloyd's of London

Royal Exchange

Bank of England

Mansion House

London Bridge

Guildhall

Armourers' Hall

Poultry

Cheapside

THE CITY OF LONDON

New Change

☀ 7a

Outward Journey

Museum of London

St Paul's Cathedral

St Paul's Churchyard

Queen Victoria Street

Golden Hinde II

Southwark Bridge

River Thames

Shakespeare's Globe Theatre

Borough

Ludgate Hill

Fleet Street

Royal Courts of Justice

THE CITY OF LONDON · THE CITY OF LONDON · THE

Victoria Embankment

Return Journey

☀ 7b

Blackfriars Bridge

☀ 7c

Fireworks

South Bank

Southwark

Ceremonies

BEATING RETREAT

House Guards Parade, Horse Guards Road, London SW1A 2AX
+44 (0)20 7839 5323   ★   householddivision.org.uk/beating-retreat

HISTORY Beating Retreat, the major musical spectacle of London's ceremonial calendar, traces its origin to the way armies ordered their soldiers to report for evening watch. Tudor-era military manuals *Rules and Ordynaunces for the Warre* (1554) and *Theorike and Practice of Moderne Warres* (1598) describe the watch being called out by an extended beating of drums. Over the following decades, drums came to be accompanied by pipes, bugles, and on occasion by entire bands.

All regiments now part of the Household Division (the Sovereign's body-guard troops) had musicians from their establishment or shortly after. Of the Foot Guards regiments, the Grenadier and Coldstream Guards had a drummer per company at or near their inception, and hautbois (French oboe) players from the 1680s. Scots Guards had hautbois from the 1710s when they moved to London. Regimental bands were formed for the Irish and Welsh Guards within months of the regiments being raised in the early 20th century.

Both Horse Guards regiments, the Life Guards and the Royal Regiment of Horse Guards (now the Blues and Royals), had kettledrummers and trumpeters from at least 1661. Uniforms of Horse Guards musicians today feature embroidered gold-laced coats as they did then. In contrast, Foot Guards musicians wear scarlet (red) coats similar to those of their predecessors in the mid-19th century, the era when Beating Retreat achieved its current form.

DESCRIPTION Over successive evenings in early June, the Massed Bands of the Household Division perform this musical and drill display on the historic parade ground known as Horse Guards Parade. Taking part are 300 musicians, drummers and pipers: Trumpeters of the Household Cavalry (that is, of the Horse Guards), Mounted Bands of the Life Guards and the Blues and Royals, and Regimental Bands, Corps of Drums, and Pipes and Drums of the Foot Guards.

Beating Retreat formally starts when the Queen (or another reviewing dignitary) steps onto the saluting platform and the National Anthem is played. After she is saluted, the programme opens with martial and classical music from the 18th century to the 21st, from Mozart to modern movie scores.

There are also slow and quick marches to which musicians, on horseback and on foot, perform precision drill of increasing complexity as the evening progresses. The programme reaches a crescendo with the Massed Bands finale and concludes with the National Anthem. The Queen then departs after which the Massed Bands ride and march from Horse Guards Parade into the night.

VISITOR INFO 🕐 Early *Jun.* 💷 Tickets from £15. Tickets are available for sale from *Jan.* Credit card payments can be made by calling +44 (0)20 7839 5323 9am-4pm *Mo-Fr.* 🚻 Toilets 🎵 Other military musical events in central London are the Easter Choral Concert (householddivision.org.uk/easter-choral-concert), and the Scarlet and Gold Concert (householddivision.org.uk/scarlet-and-gold). The latter concert is held in early *Dec.*

CEREMONY OF THE KEYS
Tower of London, London EC3N 4AB
hrp.org.uk/TowerOfLondon/WhatsOn/theceremonyofthekeys

HISTORY This is the world's oldest continuously-performed military ceremony.

Over nine and a half centuries since its founding, the Tower of London has been a fortress, a royal palace, a jail, an armoury, an arms factory, and a Jewel House. Today its role housing the Crown Jewels continues as does its status as an irreplaceable part of Britain's heritage. It has therefore always been vital to safeguard the Tower, especially to secure its gates for the night.

As part of the 13th century reorganisation of the Tower's main entrance, Middle and Byward Towers were built along the Thames. The nightly procedure for securing their gates developed into the Ceremony of the Keys. We know from a document dated 1555 that by at least then two bodies took part in the ceremony as they do now: the Tower's military guard and its Yeoman Warders.

DESCRIPTION Every evening in a brief ritual, the Tower of London is secured by the Chief Yeoman Warder accompanied by an escort from the Tower guard.

The Tower's traditional locking-up ceremony commences at 9.53pm. The Chief Yeoman Warder leaves his residence in Byward Tower and walks down Water Lane in the Outer Ward with a lantern in one hand and the Queen's Keys in the other. Waiting for him under Bloody Tower is his escort.

Flanked by the escort, the Chief Yeoman Warder walks back along Water Lane, through Byward Tower to Middle Tower. He then locks the gate under Middle Tower. Next he locks Byward Tower's gate as his escort presents arms (salutes). Then the Chief Yeoman Warder and his escort proceed along Water Lane. As the Warder once again approaches Bloody Tower, he is challenged by a sentry calling out "Halt! Who comes there?".

The Chief Yeoman Warder replies and is allowed through Bloody Tower into the Inner Ward. On the steps west of the White Tower he and his escort are met by the officer and men of the Tower's military guard. Sword drawn, the officer orders the guard and escort to present arms. The Chief Yeoman Warder raises his Tudor Bonnet and calls out "God preserve Queen Elizabeth", and the guard and escort reply "Amen". As the Tower bell sounds ten, a bugler plays Last Post and the ceremony is complete.

VISITOR INFO ☀ 9.53pm daily. Ticket-holders should be outside Middle Tower just before 9.30pm. 🅐 £5 donation suggested. 🅕 None 🅖 Apply for tickets online at least three months in advance.

CHANGING THE GUARD (BUCKINGHAM PALACE)
Buckingham Palace, Buckingham Palace Road, London SW1A 1AA
householddivision.org.uk/changing-the-guard

HISTORY The most famous guard mounting is Changing the Queen's Guard for Buckingham and St James's Palaces outside Buckingham Palace. The guard is usually provided by Foot Guards regiments, the oldest of which have been protecting London's royal palaces since the early 1660s.

For over three and a half centuries, the only time the British Foot Guards were not primarily responsible for the palaces was the decade following the Glorious Revolution of 1688. The revolution replaced James II with William III and a system of constitutional monarchy that continues to this day. Invited to safeguard England's liberties from James, William Prince of Orange and his Dutch army landed in England on 5 November 1688. Reinforced by English allies they marched on London. Wishing to avoid bloodshed, James ordered his English Guards not to resist as 3,000 Dutch Foot Guards occupied the city.

On the night of 17 December 1688, in what one historian describes as the "most momentous Changing the Guard in English history", Dutch Blue Guards replaced Coldstream Guards at Whitehall and St James's Palaces. The next morning James left London forever. His English Guards then also left the city, and their Dutch counterparts took over their London quarters and duties.

Within months the English Guards returned to spend the next decade serving their new king, William III, alongside Dutch Guards in London and in the War of the Grand Alliance (1689-1797). When the war ended, the Dutch Guards departed England by order of the English Parliament and over William's objections. Despite this quarrel, William III remained faithful to the Declaration of Right, his agreement with Parliament that made it England's ruling power.

Since the late 17th century, the only non-British troops to guard London's palaces have been Commonwealth servicemen (once every few years on special occasions). It is more usual to see other British units providing the Queen's Guard when required by Foot Guards' operational commitments. Of course, the troops performing the ceremony on most days remain the Foot Guards.

DESCRIPTION Changing the Queen's Guard is a 45-minute handover of duties between the Old and New Guards starting at 11.30am in Buckingham Palace's forecourt. While this exchange is the best known part of the ceremony, pageantry commences at 11am and finishes an hour and a half later. Note that exact times may vary for this and all ceremonies in this guide.

At 11am, the Buckingham Palace detachment of the Old Guard is inspected. Also at 11am the Guard's St James's Palace detachment forms up in the palace's Friary Court off Marlborough Road, is inspected by the Captain of the Old Guard, and salutes its Regimental Colour (flag). It then quick marches with its Regimental Colour (usually led by a Corps of Drums) along Marlborough Road and The Mall to Buckingham Palace.

Also soon after 11am, the New Guard follows a similar procedure on Wellington Barracks' parade ground. After saluting its Colour, the New Guard led by its band quick marches to Buckingham Palace. Upon its arrival in the forecourt at 11.30am, the Changing the Guard ceremony commences.

With Old and New Guards facing each other, the Regimental Band plays the New Guard's Regimental Slow March as that Guard advances towards the Old Guard. Both guards then halt and salute. The Captain of the Old Guard symbolically hands over the palace keys to the Captain of the New Guard along with responsibility for the palace's security. Officers and senior non-commissioned officers (NCOs) of both guards then march to Buckingham Palace's guardroom to complete the handover. Meanwhile the Regimental Colours of the Guards are paraded while the Band performs its musical programme.

After the handover is complete, the Regimental Band reforms and plays the Old Guard's Regimental Slow March as that Guard advances towards the New Guard. The band followed by the Old Guard then slow marches out of the forecourt, breaking into a quick march outside the palace gates.

As the Old Guard marches to Wellington Barracks, the New Guard's Buckingham Palace detachment retires to the guardroom. The St James's Palace detachment, led by its Corps of Drums, departs the forecourt by 12:15pm for Friary Court. By 12:30pm, this detachment has retired within St James's Palace.

VISITOR INFO 🌞 *Apr-Jul* 11.30am daily. *Aug-Mar* 11.30am alternate days 🅔 Free 🅕 Toilets, refreshments are in St James's Park and Green Park. 🅐 In very wet weather the ceremony is cancelled.

As the most popular of the Guard Mountings, thousands of spectators typically attend this ceremony. Four ways to beat the crowds are: (1) Arrive at the forecourt's centre railings before 10.45am to see the core of the ceremony. Otherwise do one or more of: (2) Be at St James's Palace before 11am and walk with the Guard to Buckingham Palace. (A disadvantage with walking with the St James's Palace detachment is that when you approach Victoria Monument your movement will be constrained by the crowd.) (3) Be at the monument's top steps at 11:15am to watch both Guards come and go. (4) Be at Wellington Barracks or St James's Palace for the end of the pageantry.

Foot Guards regiments also perform Changing the Guard at Windsor Castle 20 miles west of Buckingham Palace.

CHANGING THE GUARD (HORSE GUARDS)
House Guards, Whitehall, London SW1A 2AX
householddivision.org.uk/queen-life-guard

HISTORY Household Cavalry regiments providing the Queen's Life Guard have performed this daily ceremony since the mid-17th century.

From 1660, the Life Guard was posted at the Guard House of Whitehall Palace. Whitehall had been the primary royal residence since 1530 when Henry VIII took it from Cardinal Wolsey. In 1663 Charles II had the first Horse Guards building built there at the location the Commonwealth's Lord Protector, Oliver Cromwell, had stabled his guard the decade before. Although the Court moved to St James's Palace after fire destroyed most of Whitehall in 1698, the Life Guard stayed at what was still St James's only official entrance.

The Sovereign's horse-mounted guards later gave their name to Horse Guards Parade (the new parade ground west of the Guard House), and to Horse Guards Building (the new building constructed 1750-1753 on the site of the old Guard House). Today the building remains the official entrance to St James's and Buckingham Palaces, and is manned by the Life Guard. The only regular occasion now when the Horse Guards do not provide the Queen's Life Guard is in August when they are relieved by the King's Troop, Royal Horse Artillery.

DESCRIPTION Every day at Horse Guards, the Queen's Life Guard is mounted by alternate squadrons of the Household Cavalry Mounted Regiment: the Life Guards, and the Blues and Royals. As with Changing the Queen's Guard at Buckingham Palace, the 25-minute Changing the Queen's Life Guard at Horse Guards is the core of a larger spectacle. (Timings below are from Monday to Saturday. Sunday timings are one hour earlier.)

At 10.30am, the New Guard departs Hyde Park Barracks in Knightsbridge and rides via Wellington Arch, down Constitution Hill, past Buckingham Palace, along The Mall arriving at Horse Guards at 11am. Awaiting its arrival is the Old Guard, formed up for the ceremony on Horse Guards Parade in summer, and Horse Guards Building's courtyard in winter.

The New Guard forms up facing the Old. After exchanging salutes, the officer and senior NCOs of both guards retire to the guardroom to complete the handover. Once completed, the Old Guard rides along The Mall, past Buckingham Palace, up Constitution Hill, returning to its barracks by noon.

VISITOR INFO 🕐 11am *Mo-Sa*, 10am *Su* 💷 Free 🚻 Toilets are close by the Guards Memorial across Horse Guards Road as are refreshments.

CHARLES I COMMEMORATION
Banqueting House, Whitehall, London SW1A 2ER
ecws.org.uk

HISTORY "... this Court doth adjudge that he, the said Charles Stuart, as a tyrant, traitor, murderer, and public enemy to the good people of this nation, shall be put to death by the severing of his head from his body." With these words, on 27 January 1649, Parliament's High Court ruled against Charles I.

Charles I's negotiations a year earlier enticing Scotland to invade England was the reason of his trial, but the root cause was his disregard for Parliament's authority. After the death of his father James I (the first king of both England and Scotland) in 1625, Charles clashed with Parliament over taxation and its attempted impeachment of his favourite, the Duke of Buckingham. Frustrated, Charles jailed key Parliamentarians and dissolved Parliament in 1629. Lack of money for a war against Scotland forced him to recall Parliament in April 1640.

Charles dissolved this new Parliament after three weeks but England's defeat by the Scots compelled him to recall Parliament again in November 1640. The next few days saw Parliament impeach the king's new favourite, the Earl of Strafford. Charles's relationship with Parliament deteriorated further after the Earl was executed and taxation bills were passed against the king's wishes.

Reacting to the House of Commons passing the Militia Bill (taking control of the army and navy) in December 1641, Charles tried to arrest five Members of Parliament for treason but was instead forced to flee an increasingly hostile London. By March 1642 both Charles and Parliament were raising armies. The first major battle of the First English Civil War was fought at Edgehill in October.

Although Charles secured the West of the country in 1643, Parliament gained the North in 1644 with the help of the Scots, and in 1645 fielded the New Model Army. Commanded by Sir Thomas Fairfax with Oliver Cromwell as his General of Horse, the professional New Model Army beat Charles's army at Naseby in June. It then spent the next year destroying the remaining Royalist armies and garrisons. In May 1646, Charles surrendered.

The Second English Civil War broke out in 1648 with Royalist rebellions across England and Wales, and a Scottish invasion. Fairfax suppressed the English Royalists while Cromwell, after dealing with the Welsh, defeated the Scots. By the end of August the rebellion was over. Parliament was in no mood to be so forgiving a second time and Charles was put on trial for his life.

On a cold Tuesday three days after the judgment against him, Charles was taken from St James's Palace to Whitehall Palace. There, on 30 December 1649 at 2pm in front of the Banqueting Hall, the sentence was carried out.

DESCRIPTION Each year on the last Sunday in January, the King's Army (the Royalist contingent of the English Civil War Society) remembers Charles I's death by solemnly marching from St James's Palace at 11.30am to the Banqueting House at Whitehall, the route taken by Charles before his execution.

Taking part in the procession are hundreds of reenactors equipped and attired as Royalist troops from the 1640s. Reenactors are organised into contingents of cavalrymen, musketeers and pikemen. Upon arriving at Whitehall a parade is held. At noon Charles I is remembered in a wreath laying and short service. The King's Army then marches past the statue of Charles I at Trafalgar Square, through Admiralty Arch and down The Mall to St James's Palace.

VISITOR INFO 11.30am the last *Su* in *Jan*. Free Toilets, drinking fountains, refreshments in St James's Park. Also commemorating Charles I's death is the Society of King Charles the Martyr (skcm.org/feast-of-s-charles).

COMBINED CAVALRY PARADE
Hyde Park, London W2
theroyallancers.org/events [then navigate to second *Su* in *May* on calendar]

HISTORY Julius Caesar provides the earliest record of British cavalry by describing Celtic horsemen and charioteers, "a class of warriors of whom it is their practice to make great use in their battles", opposing the landing of Roman legions during his first raid on the island (55 BC). While horsemen and chariots were also prominent in opposing the Roman invasion of AD 43, the next millennium saw cavalry play a minor role in warfare on the British Isles. The Norman victory over the Saxons at Hastings in 1066 heralded a dramatic change in the use and status of cavalry. Heavily-armoured and horse-mounted feudal knights became key to England's military and social order for half a millennium.

Feudalism and the place of the mounted knight then waned in the Tudor era with the increasing influence of centralised government on society and of firearms on military tactics. This shift culminated in the formation of the New Model Army's professional cavalry regiments (1645), partially-armoured and firearms-equipped.

Cavalry regiments then saw little change in organisation and use for more than two and a half centuries. Even though this era is best remembered for Britain's red-coated infantry – Wellington's "Invincibles" in the Napoleonic Wars and Campbell's "Thin Red Line" in the Crimea – it was during this age that British cavalry celebrated its most famous actions: the Charge of the Scots Greys at Waterloo (1815), and the Charge of the Light Brigade at Balaclava (1854).

While British and Commonwealth cavalry continued their traditional role into the next century on the First World War's secondary fronts (notably across the Middle East), many cavalry regiments fought on the Western Front in a dismounted role. Their casualties over those four years rivaled the sum of cavalry casualties over the previous centuries.

To commemorate their sacrifices during the war, a memorial to cavalrymen was designed for Hyde Park. Its centrepiece was a bronze statue of a medieval knight in plate armour, sword raised, on horseback. 1924, the year of its unveiling, saw the first annual Combined Cavalry Parade.

DESCRIPTION This 30-minute parade, also known as the Cavalry Memorial Parade, comprises a short march followed by a service. While the service is closed to the public, the march can be seen from south of Serpentine Road.

The march is led by a military band followed by dismounted Household Cavalry officers and guardsmen in parade uniform with swords drawn. They are followed by thousands of serving and retired cavalrymen, young and old, marching in divisions. Although some men in the divisions are Chelsea Pensioners in their traditional tricorn hats and red coats, most are dressed in City suits. Many of those in suits also wear black bowler hats and carry furled umbrellas, off-duty attire for officers before the First World War.

Interspersed between the divisions are regimental bands in historic uniforms. Foreign military dignitaries are next to the reviewing stand in front of the Cavalry Memorial. On the reviewing stand to receive the salute is a member of the Royal Family. After all divisions have marched past, a short memorial service is held for invited guests at the Bandstand.

VISITOR INFO 🌀 11am second *Su* in *May*. 🅰 Free 🚻 Toilets are near the Bandstand in southeastern Hyde Park. Nearby are refreshments and the Dell Restaurant. 👁 Most spectators crowd opposite the reviewing stand. A better location is where the procession turns from the Broadwalk onto Serpentine Road.

LORD MAYOR'S SHOW
Mansion House, London EC4N 8BH
to and from
Royal Courts of Justice, The Strand, London WC2A 2LL
lordmayorsshow.london

HISTORY A tradition dating to 1215, the Lord Mayor's Show celebrates the City of London's self-government as well as its allegiance to the Sovereign.

John I recognized the City's self-government (including the right of its guilds to select the Mayor) in the Magna Carta (1215). The right was conditional on the newly elected mayor travelling to Westminster to show himself and swear loyalty to the Sovereign, the origin of the Lord Mayor's Show.

It did not take long for the mayor's journey to evolve into a festive occasion. The earliest known civic show was in 1236 during the reign of Henry III. The show grew with the prominence of London's mayor in the nation's life.

One of the most famous mayors was the Fishmongers Guild's William Walworth. As mayor, Walworth unsuccessfully defended London Bridge against the Peasant's Revolt on June 13, 1381. Two day later, he escorted the 14-year-old Richard II to parley with the rebels at Smithfield northwest of the City. There, in front of the rebel army and his king, Walworth attacked and mortally wounded the rebel leader, Wat Tyler. The mayor then organised loyal troops from London and nearby counties to crush the revolt.

Over time, London's loyal troops turned out for the show to complement the longstanding participation of its guilds. Archives of the oldest unit, the Honourable Artillery Company (HAC), refer to it taking part in the mid-17th century. In all likelihood the HAC and similar military fraternities were part of the show decades if not centuries before then.

Now a regiment in the Territorial Army, the HAC provides a band and marching detachment in modern uniforms and two historic units for the show. One of the historic units is the Company of Pikemen and Musketeers. Dressed as soldiers of the English Civil War, the company escorts the Lord Mayor's Coach. Escorting the Lady Mayoress is the other HAC historic unit, the Light Cavalry, in late 19th century attire. By tradition, the escort of the outgoing Lord Mayor is provided by partizan-armed Yeoman Warders of the Tower of London.

DESCRIPTION The Lord Mayor's Show is the most important ceremonial event in the City of London. Two dozen carriages, the same number of bands, over five dozen floats, and thousands of people take part in the three-mile-long procession accompanying the Lord Mayor in his gilded State Coach. Of around 150 entries in the Show, dozens are military bands and marching contingents in modern and historical uniforms, on foot, on horseback, and in armoured and other motor vehicles. Participation by 2,000 servicemen and women makes the show the capital's largest military display surpassing even Trooping the Colour.

Although the procession begins at Guildhall, the Show officially commences at 11am when the head of the parade departs Mansion House watched by the Lord Mayor. Just over an hour later, the Lord Mayor joins the procession near its tail. Following a carriage ride down Poultry, Cheapside, New Change, and St Paul's Church Yard he stops at St Paul's Cathedral to be blessed by the

Dean (the head of St Paul's governing body). The Lord Mayor's journey then continues along Ludgate Hill and Fleet Street until he arrives at the Royal Courts of Justice in Westminster at 12.30pm. There he swears allegiance to the Queen.

At 1pm the procession begins its return journey to the City from Temple Place. As with his journey to the Royal Courts of Justice, the Lord Mayor joins the parade near its tail an hour later. Proceeding by way of Victoria Embankment and Queen Victoria Street, the procession passes Mansion House and continues to Guildhall. Upon reaching Mansion House at 2.30pm, the Lord Mayor is welcomed by the Corporation of London. At 5.15pm, fireworks commence from a barge on the River Thames near Temple Place drawing the Show to a close for another year.

VISITOR INFO Second *Sa* of *Nov.* Free except for grandstand tickets at St Paul's (£39 each). Buy tickets online through the official website. Toilets, refreshments and shops are located throughout the City. Because half-a-million spectators line the route, secure a viewing spot by 10am. The best free location is at the corner of St Paul's Churchyard and New Change.

Major General's Annual Inspection of the Household Cavalry Mounted Regiment
Hyde Park, London W2
army.mod.uk/armoured/regiments/28071.aspx

HISTORY The Household Cavalry consists to two administrative regiments, the Life Guards and the Blues and Royals, and two operational regiments, the Household Cavalry Regiment and the Household Cavalry Mounted Regiment.

Two squadrons from the Life Guards and two from the Blues and Royals form the Windsor-based Household Cavalry Regiment. When assigned to this operational regiment, cavalrymen are dressed in camouflage uniforms, and ride Scimitar (reconnaissance) and Spartan (support/anti-armor/command) armoured fighting vehicles. Their duties are primarily battlefield reconnaissance.

When not part of the armored Household Cavalry Regiment, cavalrymen are assigned to the Household Cavalry Mounted Regiment. On duty they are dressed in glittering armour and ride horses. Their duties are mainly ceremonial. One squadron from the Life Guards and one from the Blues and Royals form the London-based regiment headquartered at Hyde Park Barracks in Knightsbridge (the Household Cavalry's home since 1795).

DESCRIPTION This inspection of the Household Cavalry Mounted Regiment takes place in Hyde Park off South Carriage Drive opposite Hyde Park Barracks. Its purpose is to ensure the regiment meets the exacting standards expected of it for the upcoming ceremonial season.

Conducting the inspection is the General Officer Commanding London District. This senior officer is also the Major General Commanding the Household Division (the two Horse Guards and five Foot Guards regiments). During the parade, the Household Cavalry Mounted Regiment walks and trots past the General Officer Commanding London District while accompanied by the Mounted Bands of the Life Guards and the Blues and Royals.

VISITOR INFO 10am on a *Th* in late *Mar* Free None Hyde Park has been used for military ceremonies since at least the reign of James II (1680s).

REMEMBRANCE SUNDAY CENOTAPH PARADE
The Cenotaph, Whitehall, London SW1
www.britishlegion.org.uk/remembrance/how-we-remember/remembrance-sunday

HISTORY Four years of trench warfare on the First World War's Western Front is recognized as among the bloodiest combat in history. Of those years, the last was especially desperate. On the Eastern Front, Communists took over Russia and in March 1918 signed the (peace) Treaty of Brest-Litovsk with Imperial Germany. 60 German divisions hurriedly redeployed to the Western Front made deep advances almost to the Channel ports. But the Allies hung on and by autumn counter-offensives on the front and revolutionary agitation at the rear pushed the German Army to the point of collapse. At 11am on 11 November 1918 the Armistice suspended fighting. By that time 5.7 million British and Commonwealth soldiers had fought in the war and 700,000 had been killed.

On 19 July 1919, the British Empire's Victory Parade was held at Whitehall where a temporary plaster cenotaph (from the Greek for "empty tomb") had been erected. Re-erected in stone as a permanent memorial, the Cenotaph was unveiled on 11 November 1920 to coincide with the entombment at Westminster Abbey of the Unknown Soldier from the Western Front. A year later the first annual Armistice Day ceremony was held at the Cenotaph.

Following the Second World War, the scope of the ceremony expanded to commemorate the fallen from both World Wars and the observance was re-named Remembrance Day. The Cenotaph, now a memorial to all those who died serving Britain and her Commonwealth, stands in the middle of Whitehall between Downing Street and King Charles Street flanked by flags of Britain's armed forces. Engraved in Roman numerals are the dates of the World Wars along with the simple dedication "The Glorious Dead".

DESCRIPTION Remembrance Sunday Cenotaph Parade's focus is two minutes of silence from 11am.

A few minutes before 11am, the Queen arrives at the Cenotaph joining British and other Commonwealth leaders. Formed around them as a hollow square are ex-servicemen and women organised by the Royal British Legion; detachments from the Royal Navy, the Royal Marines, the Royal Air Force, and their counterpart auxiliary, nursing and merchant navy services; detachments of the King's Troop, Royal Horse Artillery, Household Cavalry, Foot Guards and other Army units; and bands of the Royal Marines, Guards Division and Royal Air Force. The public lines the pavement on both sides of Whitehall. At this stage most detachments have been in place, and bands have been performing, for half an hour. Bands cease playing and the crowd falls silent as 11am approaches.

As Big Ben sounds 11, the start of two minutes silence is marked by the King's Troop, Royal Horse Artillery firing a single gun on Horse Guards Parade. After the end of the silence is marked in the same way, buglers sound Last Post.

The Queen then lays a wreath of poppies at the foot of the Cenotaph. She is followed in this by other members of the Royal Family, parliamentary leaders, High Commissioners (ambassadors) from Commonwealth countries, and by the heads of British armed and civilian services. Next, the Lord Bishop of London leads a short service. At the service's end, trumpeters play The Rouse (a short Reveille), and the National Anthem is sung completing the official ceremony.

From 11.15am the Queen and senior dignitaries file into the Foreign and Commonwealth Office west of the Cenotaph. Veterans then lay their wreaths at the Cenotaph. At 11.30am a marchpast commences of 10,000 former servicemen and women to the sound of military bands. The parade passes the Cenotaph, proceeds through Parliament Square then via Horse Guards Road to Horse Guards Parade where it marches past the reviewing stand. The march takes an hour to complete bringing the parade to a close at 12.30pm.

VISITOR INFO ❄ 11am on Remembrance Sunday, closest *Su* to 11 *Nov.* ⏍ Free ⏍ Toilets at Westminster station and St James's Park. Refreshments in St James's Park near Westminster station and at the northern end of Whitehall. ⏍ This is the most crowded London ceremony. Be there by 9am to secure a good position. The best location to view the parade is northwest of the Cenotaph.

Royal Gun Salutes (Royal Parks)
Green Park, London SW1 ★ Hyde Park, London W2
royal.gov.uk/RoyalEventsandCeremonies/GunSalutes/Gunsalutes.aspx

HISTORY On a dozen occasions annually at one of two royal parks, gun salutes are performed in a mark of respect originating in medieval Europe.

Since ancient times subordinates have saluted their superiors to show respect and trust. Modern salutes trace their origin directly to medieval Europe: hand salutes started from lifting a helmet's visor, sword salutes from lifting a sword's hilt to the lips (representing kissing the Holy Cross), rifle salutes pointing a firearm upwards where it was not a danger. All these actions place the person initiating the salute at a disadvantage to the person receiving it to show they mean no harm. The origin of gun salutes is no different.

Invented in early 14th century Europe, firearms were initially employed in siege and naval warfare due to their massive weight. To show they meant no harm, warships would fire their guns in a salute prior to entering port, making their primary weapons temporarily ineffective. By the early 18th century, Royal Navy regulations determined when gun salutes were required.

Royal gun salutes were incorporated into regulations of the Royal Artillery. Formed as two permanent companies at Woolwich in 1716 and expanded in 1722 to become the Royal Regiment of Artillery, the Royal Artillery replaced the Army's civilian gunners. Civilian artillery drivers were next to go when the Royal Horse Artillery (RHA) was raised to provide cavalry with fire support in 1793. RHA gunners and drivers were horse mounted until the 1930s when their troops were mechanised. George VI requested one of their troops take part in London ceremonial events dressed in historic uniforms. His request was fulfilled in 1947 when the Riding Troop was renamed the King's Troop.

DESCRIPTION Royal Gun Salutes in both Hyde Park and Green Park involve the same gunners, horses, guns, and number of rounds fired. All gunners, wearing Napoleonic-era uniforms, are from the King's Troop, RHA. Dozens of horses, ridden either singly or by one gunner on a pair of horses with three pairs hitched towing each gun, are part of the ceremony. The six guns firing the salute are 13-pounders, field artillery pieces first used by the RHA in 1904. The number of rounds fired by each gun is 41 (21 for a basic Royal Gun Salute plus an extra 20 because the salute is fired in a royal park).

However, despite identical gunners, horses, guns, and number of rounds, the differences in topography between the parks make each of the Royal Gun Salutes distinct. In Hyde Park a few minutes before noon, six gun teams form up line abreast and gallop from the north down the eastern side of the park through the expanse known as the Parade Ground. Upon reaching the firing line, they rapidly unlimber the guns and prepare them for firing while their horses are swiftly retired and reformed well behind the firing line.

At the specified time, the order is given for Number 1 Gun to fire. It does so with an explosion and plenty of white smoke. The other guns fire in turn at set intervals. The sequence is repeated with Number 1 Gun until all 41 rounds are discharged. Horses are then swiftly brought forward, guns rapidly re-limbered, and the teams gallop away in as spectacular a manner as they arrived.

For the Royal Gun Salute at Green Park, the six gun teams form up in single file along Constitution Hill between Buckingham Palace and Green Park. A few minutes before the allotted time, still in single file, they cross over into Green Park and gallop a short distance until they form up line abreast on the firing line facing north. The same procedure of unlimbering, horses to the rear, firing in sequence, horses returning, relimbering and galloping away is performed in the narrower confines of the park.

Although the firing sequence only takes 10 minutes, it is worthwhile attending from 15 minutes before the first round is fired to hear a performance by the King's Troop musicians.

VISITOR INFO Green Park 🎖 12.52pm on the *Sa* in *mid-Jun* of the Queen's Birthday Parade, around 11.10am on the *Nov* weekday of the State Opening of Parliament. Royal Gun Salutes also occur for Royal births, deaths and marriages, when visiting Heads of State meet the Queen, and also when the Queen closes a Parliamentary session. 💷 Free 🚻 Toilets are in Green Park as are refreshments. **Hyde Park** 🎖 Noon on the following Royal anniversaries: 6 *Feb* for the Queen's Accession Day, 21 *Apr* for the Queen's Birthday, 2 *Jun* for the Queen's Coronation Day, 10 *Jun* celebrating Prince Philip's Birthday (sometimes held at Green Park), 14 *Nov* for the Prince of Wales's birthday 💷 Free 🚻 Disabled and other toilets are at a number of locations in Hyde Park including near the Bandstand in the park's southeastern quadrant. Also in the quadrant are refreshments and the Dell Restaurant. 🚇 After viewing the noon ceremony, a 1pm Royal Gun Salute can be seen at the Tower of London. Catch the Piccadilly line from Hyde Park Corner to South Kensington then change to the District or Circle line travelling east to Tower Hill. After a brisk walk from Tower Hill, you should arrive in time to view the Royal Gun Salute at the Tower of London. **General Note Applying to Royal Gun Salutes at Green Park, Hyde Park and at the Tower of London**

The very loud noise from these events may make them unsuitable for young children or pets. Also, since the guns emit lots of smoke, be sure to stay upwind of them. Regardless of location, if a ceremony's date falls on a Sunday, the Royal Gun Salute takes place the next day instead. When Elizabeth II is succeeded as Sovereign, most dates on which Royal Gun Salutes are performed will change.

☀ 11 ROYAL GUN SALUTES (TOWER OF LONDON)
Tower of London, London EC3N 4AB
royal.gov.uk/RoyalEventsandCeremonies/GunSalutes/Gunsalutes.aspx

HISTORY The earliest recorded Royal Gun Salute at the Tower of London was in 1533 celebrating Anne Boleyn's marriage to Henry VIII. (Boleyn's failure to produce a male heir - she gave birth to the future Elizabeth I instead - led to a visit to the Tower three years later and her beheading on Tower Green.) Since then Royal Gun Salutes at the Tower have been conducted on Tower Wharf.

Although Tower Wharf predates Henry's reign by over two centuries, his navy is best known for using it to transfer guns, gunpowder and ammunition from the Tower's stores to his warships. *Mary Rose*, Henry's famous but ill-starred flagship, sailed to London for that purpose in 1511 following her launch at Portsmouth. It may have been during this time of naval expansion that Royal Gun Salutes, already used by warships, were adopted at the Tower.

During the 16th century, Tower gunners were part-time civilian employees. They became full-time civilian employees in the 1680s, soldiers in the Royal Artillery the following century, and stayed at the Tower until 1924. In that year the Honourable Artillery Company (HAC) replaced them in their main ceremonial duty: performing Royal Gun Salutes from Tower Wharf.

DESCRIPTION Royal Gun Salutes at the Tower of London have a more modern appearance than those at London's royal parks. Gunners' uniforms, their means of transport (Army light trucks), and their guns (L118 105mm Light Guns in service since 1976) are contemporary. This outward modernity belies the fact that the Royal Gun Salute at the Tower is the older ceremony, and that the unit providing its gunners, the HAC, is older than that providing the royal parks' gunners by more than four centuries.

At 12.45pm, the HAC detachment drives along the western side of the Tower of London. Passing Middle Tower, the convoy turns left onto Tower Wharf and halts. Its four guns are readied for action at the gun park between the Queen's Stairs on Tower Wharf and the postern (small gate) by Middle Tower.

At 1pm the guns open fire one after the other. On royal anniversaries the salute lasts 15 minutes as 62 rounds are fired (21 for a basic Royal Gun Salute plus an extra 20 because the salute is fired in a royal fortress plus another 21 for the City of London). On other occasions the salute lasts 10 minutes as 41 rounds are fired (the number comprised as above minus the rounds for the City).

Once the last round is fired, the guns are rehitched and towed through the City of London to the HAC's home at Finsbury Barracks.

VISITOR INFO 🌑 62-gun Royal Gun Salutes take place at 1pm on: 6 *Feb* for the Queen's Accession Day, 21 *Apr* for the Queen's Birthday, 2 *Jun* for the Queen's

Coronation Day, 10 *Jun* for Prince Philip's Birthday, *Sa* mid-*Jun* for the Queen's official Birthday, 14 *Nov* for the Prince of Wales's birthday. 41-gun Royal Salutes take place at noon for State Visits and the State Opening of Parliament. Salutes are also performed for visits by Heads of State (41-gun) and for Royal occasions (62-gun) including births, deaths and marriages. ⓔ Free ⓕ Toilets near the Welcome Centre to the west of the Tower. ◍ See the previous entry's Note.

STATE OPENING OF PARLIAMENT
House of Lords, United Kingdom Parliament, London SW1A 0PW
householddivision.org.uk/state-opening-of-parliament

HISTORY Parliament gradually developed from the Curia Regis (Latin for the "Royal Council") of England's Norman Kings. As the king spent much of his reign inspecting the kingdom, he chose the place the Curia and its successor, the House of Lords, would convene for Parliament. During the reigns of Henry II and Henry III, the Palace of Westminster became the main royal residence, and government increasingly came to be based there. By the end of the 13th century, Parliament (including the House of Commons) was also at Westminster.

A century later and the protocols for the State Opening of Parliament were well established. In accord with the status of its two houses, the ceremony took place in the House of Lords where the Sovereign was enthroned. The Commons were summoned there to hear the address opening the Parliamentary session. While the protocols remain in place today, the relationship between the three constituent parts of Parliament - Sovereign, Lords and Commons - has changed dramatically over the intervening period.

When fire destroyed Westminster Palace, Henry VIII moved his court to Whitehall Palace. Increased autonomy for Parliamentary, judicial and administrative functions that stayed at Westminster was enhanced by Henry's "break with Rome". Henry bolstered Parliament's authority by having it pass acts dealing with the line of succession (1534), dissolution of monasteries (1536), and abolition of chantries (religious trust funds, 1545).

More dramatic events and changes occurred under the Stuart kings. First was the thwarted attempt to blow up James I and the House of Lords during the 1605 State Opening of Parliament. The failed Gunpowder Plot is memorialized in Guy Fawkes Night fireworks (5 November), and in the Yeomen of the Guard searching the palace's cellars prior to each State Opening of Parliament.

Then in 1642 James I's son, Charles I, entered the House of Commons to arrest five Parliamentarians. No monarch has entered the Commons since. Now, when the Sovereign's messenger tries to summons the Commons to the Lords during the State Opening, the door is slammed in his face. When the Commons finally hear his summons, they proceed to the Lords at a relaxed pace.

DESCRIPTION This ceremony's centrepiece is the Queen's Speech in the House of Lords. The focus of this entry, however, is the Queen's ceremonial procession from Buckingham Palace to Westminster Palace.

The procession's route is from Buckingham Palace along The Mall, onto Horse Guards Road and Horse Guards Parade, through Horse Guards Arch onto

Whitehall, past the Cenotaph, down Parliament Street and Parliament Square to Westminster Palace. Lining the route are Household Division troops as well as other members of the armed forces.

At 10.20am, Foot Guards from Wellington Barracks arrive outside Buckingham Palace. They will take part in Changing the Queen's Guard after the Queen has left the palace. Concurrent with their arrival, a contingent of Horse Guards rides into Buckingham Palace for duty escorting the Regalia: the Imperial State Crown, Mace and Sword of State normally secured within the Tower of London. Royal carriages to transport the Regalia arrive a few minutes later.

At 10.40am, the Regalia leave Buckingham Palace for Westminster Palace in separate horse-drawn carriages escorted by Household Cavalry. Minutes later hundreds of men and horses also from the Household Cavalry appear gleaming and clattering down Constitution Road. They ride around the Victoria Memorial disappearing into Buckingham Palace forecourt.

At 11am they reappear at the head and tail of the royal procession at the centre of which is the Queen travelling in her horse-drawn State Coach. As the royal procession proceeds down The Mall, the New and Old Guards commence Changing the Guard.

When the Queen enters the House of Lords via the Sovereign's Entrance at around 11.10am, a Royal Gun Salute is performed at Green Park by the King's Troop, Royal Horse Artillery. (At noon, the Honourable Artillery Company fires a Royal Gun Salute for the occasion at the Tower of London).

After being dressed in royal robes and the Imperial State Crown, the Queen takes her place in the House of Lords on the Throne. Acting as the Queen's messenger, the House of Lords's Sergeant at Arms-equivalent known as Black Rod then walks to the House of Commons to summons its members. By tradition, the doors to the Commons are slammed in his face and it is only after he knocks on the door three times with his mace that the door is reopened so the members can hear the summons.

Once representative members of the House of Commons have made their way to the House of Lords, the Queen gives a short speech (the Speech from the Throne) provided to her by the government outlining its legislative programme during the coming Session of Parliament. At the end of the speech, the Session is formally open. The Queen departs Westminster Palace at 12.15pm for Buckingham Palace travelling the reverse of the route she took that morning.

VISITOR INFO 🌸 A late morning on a weekday in early-to-mid *Nov*. The ceremony also takes place with the same timings after General Elections. 🌸 Free 🌸 Toilets, refreshments in St James's Park. 🌸 The procession is best viewed near Victoria Memorial in front of Buckingham Palace.

TRAFALGAR PARADE
Trafalgar Square, London WC2
+44 (0)20 7654 7015 ★ sea-cadets.org/trafalgar-day

HISTORY The Battle of Trafalgar, 21 October 1805, was the greatest naval battle of the Napoleonic Wars, and determined who ruled the seas for a century.

On 14 September 1805 Vice Admiral Horatio Nelson set sail from Portsmouth with orders to blockade or destroy the Combined French and Spanish Fleet under Vice Admiral Vielleneuve. On 19 October Vielleneuve's fleet left Cadiz while Nelson and his fleet waited unseen out to sea. On the morning of 21 October, the two fleets converged near Cape Trafalgar off southwest Spain. 41 French and Spanish warships were in line ahead forming an arc, 33 British warships deployed in two squadrons line ahead: one led by Nelson in HMS *Victory*, the other by Vice Admiral Collingwood in HMS *Royal Sovereign*.

At noon, the lines of the British Fleet speared that of the Combined Fleet cleaving the Combined formation in two. The rear third of the French and Spanish ships became trapped by Collingwood's squadron, the other two thirds hampered by Nelson's from turning back to save their comrades. A desperate battle ensued with ships ramming each other and firing broadsides at point blank range.

By the time darkness fell, the Combined Fleet had lost 16,000 men and 22 ships, the Royal Navy 1,600 men and no ships. However, numbering among the British dead was its commander. As *Victory* was locked in battle with *Redoutable*, a sniper on the French ship mortally wounded Nelson. Before he died, Nelson learned of Villeneuve's surrender aboard the French flagship *Bucentaure* and that Britain had won another battle, his greatest victory.

Nelson's body arrived at Greenwich on 23 December 1805. He lay there in the Painted Hall from 5 to 7 January 1806. His body was then entombed in St Paul's Cathedral in London where it remains today. Monuments to Nelson were constructed all over Britain, but there was no outdoor public memorial to him in London until 1843 when Nelson's Column was erected in Trafalgar Square.

DESCRIPTION On 21 October every year, commemorations are held in honour of Nelson's victory at Trafalgar. The largest commemoration is the Trafalgar Parade held on the Sunday closest to 21 October, an occasion when hundreds of Sea Cadets march to Trafalgar Square on behalf of the Royal Navy.

The event commences at 11am with the arrival of the Lord Mayor of Westminster. His arrival is followed by traditional shipboard entertainments of Nelson's day: horn pipe dancing, and club and cutlass swinging. At 11.15am the National Massed Band of the Sea Cadet Corps leads platoons of Sea and Marine Cadets onto Trafalgar Square from The Mall via Admiralty Arch. Following a performance by the band, the Colour Party with its Ceremonial Guard arrives at 11.35am.

The First Sea Lord arrives at 11.50am and inspects the parade. Wreaths are then laid at the foot of Nelson's Column by dignitaries including a representative of the French Navy. Concluding the short service that follows is the reading of Nelson's prayer before the Battle of Trafalgar.

The parade concludes with a march past of the Colour Party, Ceremonial Guard, platoons and band. These contingents then march off Trafalgar Square through Admiralty Arch and down The Mall.

VISITOR INFO 🌐 11am on the *Su* closest to 21 **Oct.** 💷 Free 🚻 Toilets are available in the middle of Trafalgar Square and in the National Gallery to its north. Refreshments are also available at the National Gallery and elsewhere around the square.

TROOPING THE COLOUR
House Guards Parade, Horse Guards Road, London SW1
householddivision.org.uk/trooping-the-colour

HISTORY Flags and similar standards played an important part in warfare for thousands of years. They were an object for soldiers to follow in the confusion of battle, rallying points in crisis, and symbols of honour in war and peace.

In Roman times, each legion had an eagle standard made of gold as well as a standard of the emperor to emphasize the link between legionnaires and their commander-in-chief. It was well over a millennium after the Roman legions departed Britain that military standards reappeared of the same permanence, accorded the same respect, and as symbolic of the relationship between Sovereign and soldiers. This time, in the mid-17th century, standards were known as Colours, brightly coloured flags of regiments in the new professional army.

Since the Royal Warrant of 1751 regiments have been allowed only two Colours. These were the Regimental Colour (featuring the regimental badge), and the Queen's Colour (a Union Jack with the title and number of the battalion at the flag's centre surmounted by St Edward's Crown). When the Sovereign is a king, the latter Color is called the King's Colour.

By mid-17th century, two ceremonies familiarised soldiers with Colours identifying their regiment: Guard Mounting, and Lodging the Colours. During the former ceremony, Colours were paraded down the regiment's ranks as part of the morning's Guard Mounting whenever the Sovereign was resident in a garrison's district. In the latter ceremony, Colours were paraded before they were lodged safely for the night. Because the music played during the Lodging was called a troop, over time the daily marching of the flag up and down the ranks became known as Trooping the Colour. Trooping the Colour was first used to celebrate the Sovereign's birthday in 1748.

DESCRIPTION In June, the King's Troop, Royal Horse Artillery and the Massed Bands and Troops of the Household Division take part in Trooping the Color, London's most spectacular military event. Also known as the Queen's Birthday Parade, the ceremony is held on the Queen's official birthday in June.

There are two public rehearsals for the parade, the Major General's Review and the Colonel's Review, held two weeks and one week before the Queen's Birthday Parade, respectively. The description that follows applies broadly to those rehearsals as it does specifically to the Queen's Birthday Parade.

At the core of the ceremony is a few minutes during which the Queen's Colour of a Foot Guards regiment is "trooped'" between ranks of the Household Division. Around these few minutes are built three hours of music, drill, and royal gun salutes.

The three hours start shortly after 10am when the Guards Division's Massed Bands and Corps of Drums march onto Horse Guards Parade. Next onto the parade ground are Foot Guards contingents. The King's Troop, Royal Horse Artillery then arrives, forming up in St James's Park.

At 11am the Queen or her representative enters Horse Guards Parade escorted by the Household Cavalry and Mounted Bands. She then inspects the Foot Guards and the Mounted Troops ranked behind them. After the Queen takes her place on the saluting platform, the Massed Bands and Drums march around Horse Guards Parade in slow and quick time.

After the bands cease playing, a lone drummer beats a call. In response, the Escort for the Colour marches to the centre of the parade ground facing the Queen's Colour. The Regimental Sergeant Major transfers the Colour from the Colour Sergeant to the Ensign of the Escort to the Colour. The Escort presents arms and the National Anthem is played.

Once the Massed Bands and Drums have executed the intricate Spin Wheel maneuver to reposition themselves, the Ensign then troops the Colour in front of the ranks of Foot Guards. As the Escort marches between the ranks, the men of the Foot Guards contingents present arms. The contingents then turn and march around the parade ground in slow time followed by another circuit in quick time, saluting the Queen as they pass her.

After the Foot Guards return to their original positions, it is the turn of the Mounted Troops (the King's Troop and the Household Cavalry) to ride past in slow and quick time. They likewise salute as they pass the Queen. Upon the Mounted Troops returning to their positions, the National Anthem and Royal Salute are performed completing the ceremonies at Horse Guards Parade.

The King's Troop is the first to leave in preparation for its Royal Gun Salute at Green Park. Next to leave are the Massed Bands who begin the march up the Mall heading the Royal Procession. The Bands are followed by the Queen in her carriage followed by the Foot Guards with the Household Cavalry in the rear.

Upon reaching Buckingham Palace, the new Queen's Guard enters the forecourt, forming up opposite the old Queen's Guard as they usually do. The Queen stands on a saluting platform in the central gateway and receives the salute as the Foot Guards and then Mounted Troops pass her. After the Queen retires within Buckingham Palace, the usual daily ceremony of Changing the Guard takes place.

At 12.52pm the King's Troop fires a 41-gun salute in Green Park, while at 1pm the Honourable Artillery Company fires a 61-gun salute at the Tower of London. Also at 1pm, the Queen appears on Buckingham Palace's balcony for a flypast by the Royal Air Force (weather permitting).

VISITOR INFO 🌐 *Jun*. Trooping the Colour commences at 11am on the first (Major General's Review), second (Colonel's Review), and third (The Queen's Birthday Parade) *Sa* in **Jun** (or as in 2016 on the last *Sa* in **May**, and the first and second *Sa* in **Jun**). 💷 £10 for Major General's and Colonel's Review, £30 for the Queen's Birthday Parade. 🚻 Toilets 🌐 The Household Division advises:

> Tickets … are allocated by ballot. Up to a maximum of 3 tickets can be applied for Trooping the Colour. The Reviews have no restriction on the number of tickets applied for … Applications should be made **in January or February only (any application other then the period stated will not be included in the ballot)**. Please write in to: Brigade Major, HQ Household Division, Horse Guards, Whitehall, London SW1A 2AX. Please enclose a self-address stamped envelope (or International Reply Coupon) in your application and do not send any money until requested to do so.

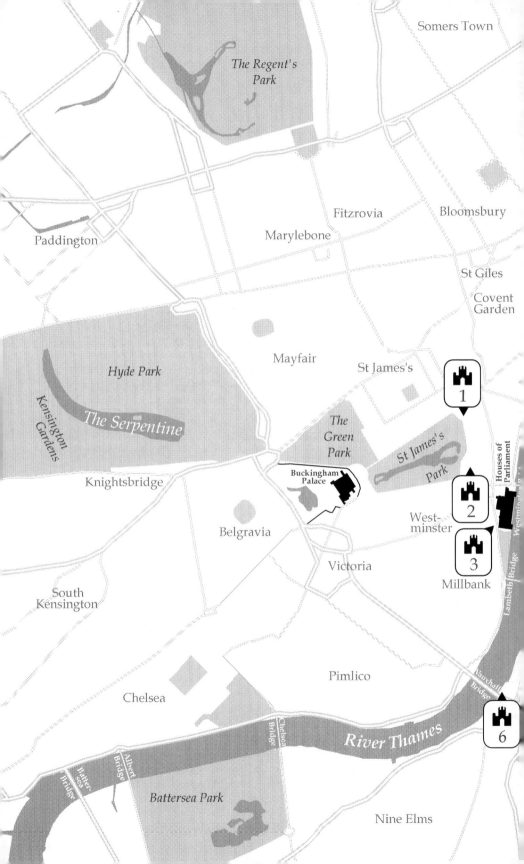

Somers Town

The Regent's Park

Fitzrovia   Bloomsbury

Marylebone

Paddington   St Giles

Covent
Garden

Mayfair   St James's

1

Hyde Park

Kensington Gardens

The Serpentine

The
Green
Park

St James's
Park

Houses of
Parliament

Buckingham
Palace

Westminster
Bridge

2

Knightsbridge

West-
minster

3

Belgravia

Millbank

Victoria

Lambeth Bridge

South
Kensington

Pimlico

Vauxhall Bridge

Chelsea

6

Chelsea Bridge

Albert Bridge

River Thames

Battersea Bridge

Battersea Park

Nine Elms

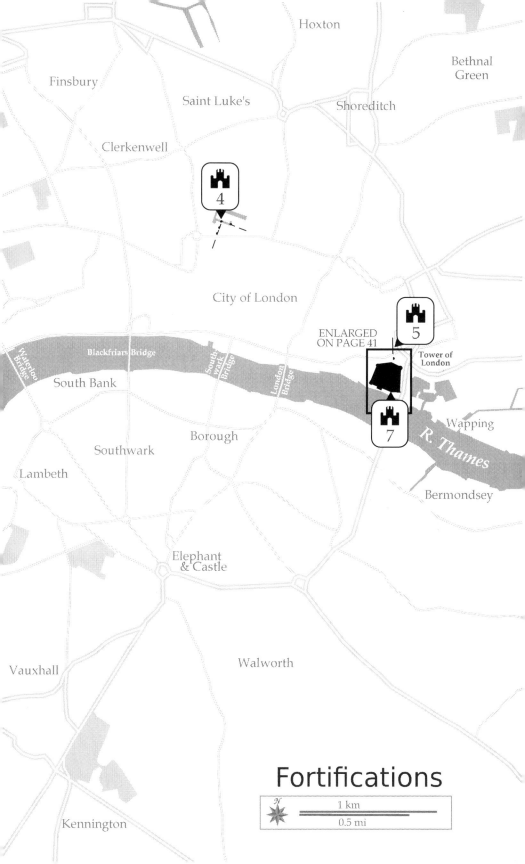

Hoxton

Bethnal
Green

Finsbury

Saint Luke's

Shoreditch

Clerkenwell

4

City of London

ENLARGED
ON PAGE 41

5

Tower of
London

Waterloo Bridge

Blackfriars Bridge

Southwark Bridge

London Bridge

South Bank

Wapping

R. Thames

Borough

7

Southwark

Lambeth

Bermondsey

Elephant
& Castle

Vauxhall

Walworth

Kennington

Fortifications

1 km

0.5 mi

Fortifications

ADMIRALTY CITADEL
Horse Guards Road, London SW1A 2PA

HISTORY Of London's Second World War defences, best known are bunkers such as the Churchill War Rooms and Underground stations that protected the nation's leadership and the city's populace, respectively. Less well known are above ground fortifications with Admiralty Citadel being the prime example.

First World War bombing raids on London by Zeppelin airships and Gotha biplanes led to the saying "the bomber would always get through". To avoid bombers striking Britain's leaders and their staffs, interwar plans were to move government departments to northwest London and the West Country in the event of war. Under 1937 plans, the Admiralty fortified its Chart Depot in the north London suburb of Cricklewood. After fortifications were completed in 1940, the plans were abandoned. In hindsight, the inconvenience of evacuation was judged to outweigh the risk of enemy bombing.

Work then started on a stronghold next to Admiralty offices at Whitehall. The site chosen was the triangle of parkland west of the Old Admiralty Building. Completed in 1941, the Citadel (described by Winston Churchill as a "vast monstrosity which weighs on the Horse Guards Parade") became the Admiralty's operations and communications centre. It was staffed for these tasks by hundreds of men and women for the rest of the war. Tunnels connected Admiralty Citadel to the Admiralty and to bunkers under Whitehall.

Bunkers and other fortifications continued to be used immediately after the war, a time widespread bomb damage meant space was at a premium. Then, from the late 1940s to the collapse of the Soviet Union, the Citadel was again a Ministry of Defence stronghold, this time for the Cold War.

DESCRIPTION Admiralty Citadel is a windowless three-story concrete block in the northeast corner of St James's Park. The building fits into the triangle enclosed by The Mall to its northwest, Horse Guards Road to its southwest, and the Old Admiralty Building (also known as the Admiralty Extension) to its east.

Admiralty Citadel's thick concrete roof was designed to provide protection against 250 kg (550 lb) bombs. Underneath the roof are three floors. The lowest floor once housed its operations centre, while the floor above contained accommodation. On the top floor were plant rooms for machinery including electricity generators.

Two passageways can be observed connecting the Citadel to the Old Admiralty Building where the Citadel's longest side runs parallel to the 19th century structure. Steps lead to an entrance on its short southern side. Here as well as on the longer western side, Virginia ivy hides much of the fortification's light brown concrete structure for most of the year making it surprisingly unobtrusive. Even so, what were originally machine gun pillboxes can still be seen on the Citadel's northwestern and southwestern corners. Least obscured is its northern side, allowing a better view of this monolith as it would have been when constructed at the height of the Second World War.

VISITOR INFO 🌐 24 hours daily (outside only) 💶 Free 🚻 Toilets are near the Guards Memorial over Horse Guards Road as are refreshments. ⚪ From 1943 to 1945, Supreme Commander of Allied Forces in Europe General Dwight Eisenhower established his headquarters at the Goodge Street Underground Station just over a mile north of Admiralty Citadel.

CHURCHILL WAR ROOMS
Clive Steps, King Charles Street, London SW1A 2AQ
+44 (0)20 7930 6961 ★ iwm.org.uk/visits/churchill-war-rooms

HISTORY Originally a basement three metres below the New Public Offices, the future Churchill War Rooms was converted in 1936 into a three-room, eighty-man bunker. During 1939, the fortification was expanded to accommodate the War Cabinet and its staff, the Chiefs of Staff and other command, planning and intelligence bodies. Activated in August, the bunker was reinforced with a one-metre-thick concrete slab over its ceiling in October, and renamed the Cabinet War Rooms in December.

Until the defeat of Japan, it protected hundreds of staff (from the Prime Minister to typists) over an area that eventually covered three acres (one and a quarter hectares) divided into 200 rooms. As it happened, there were relatively few hits in the area and no direct hits on the building. Today, the Rooms remain as they were in 1945 on the day after V-J (Victory over Japan) Day.

DESCRIPTION Near its entrance is the War Rooms' centerpiece: the Cabinet War Room with seating arrangements including for Churchill as they were near the end of the Battle of Britain (July-October 1940). The Battle of Britain was the result of the Luftwaffe (German Air Force) campaign against British air and sea targets. Fought between German Messerschmitt Bf 109 and Bf 110 fighters on one hand and British Hurricane Mk I and Spitfire Mk I fighers on the other, the battle ended with the Royal Air Force (RAF) retaining air superiority over Britain.

It was towards the end of the Battle of Britain that the German invasion of Britain, Operation Sea Lion, was postponed. Had Sea Lion gone ahead, London would have been the objective of one of two army groups, Army Group A, under Field Marshal Gerd von Rundstedt. Army Group A's initial nine-division-strong airbourne and amphibious assault on southeast England needed air superiority to stand a chance against the Royal Navy. The Luftwaffe's failure in the Battle of Britain led to Sea Lion's indefinite delay, a source of considerable relief to Churchill and his War Cabinet in the autumn of 1940.

Past the Cabinet Room is a corridor from where visitors can see sub-basement sleeping quarters. Further along the corridor is the Transatlantic Lobby where, connected to a scrambler, the first hotline was established in late 1943 to Washington, DC. The hotline allowed British Prime Minister Churchill and US President Roosevelt to talk near instantly and securely.

Through the Lobby is the Churchill Museum. The most recent part of the complex, the museum chronicles Winston Churchill's life with audio and video displays, personal mementos, correspondence, posters, quotations, photos and cartoons. Highlights are a Dervish chieftain's rifle given to him as a spoil of the Battle of Omdurman in the Sudan (1898), his trench periscope and a Colt Model 1911 semi-automatic pistol (his favourite firearm) from his service on the First World War's Western Front, his Bowker hat, and his bizarre Burgundy crushed velvet jumpsuit known as a siren suit. On a less personal note is an Enigma coding machine the decryption of which so greatly contributed to the Allied victory. At the room's centre is the Lifeline Interactive with documents, films, photographs and audio accessed using touchscreens.

After exiting the Churchill Museum, passing through the Transatlantic Lobby again and continuing down the long corridor, a set of rooms opens to the left: the Churchill Suite. The Cabinet War Rooms expanded into this area in 1941 to provide living quarters for Churchill's personal staff. After the Churchill Suite and the Switch Room Café, a point half-way along the museum, is a room where Churchill's speech of 11 September 1940 - "Every Man to His Post" - is broadcast. He made this and three other broadcasts to the nation from the War Rooms.

Next is the heart of the War Rooms complex: operations and map rooms. First are the rooms that were the Advanced Headquarters of the Home Forces at the peak of their activity when the threat of invasion was highest. Through an incision in a steel-reinforced concrete block is the Map room. It shows wall maps and pins, telephones and notices as they were in August 1945 the day after V-J (Victory over Japan) Day when the bunker was abandoned. Hanging on one of the pillars is a blackboard used during the dark days of the Battle of Britain to tally enemy aircraft shot down each day.

Providing close access to the Map Room is Churchill's bedroom next door. This room also features maps, specifically of Britain's coastal defences and the possible landing points for a potential German invasion.

VISITOR INFO 🌐 9.30am-6pm daily. Closed 24-26 *Dec* 💷 Adult £16.35, Child (5-15y) £8.15, Concession £13.05 🅕 Toilets, café, audio guides, book and gift shop 🛈 The section of the War Rooms open to the public is only a portion of a much larger facility. The War Rooms originally had a staff of up to 528 people with facilities including dormitories, a hospital, and a shooting range.

JEWEL TOWER
Abingdon Street, Westminster, London SW1P 3JX
+44 (0)20 7222 2219   ★   www.english-heritage.org.uk/visit/places/jewel-tower

HISTORY When the Saxon king St Edward the Confessor (r.1042-1066) rebuilt Westminster Abbey, he built a palace next to it. Over the centuries the Palace of

Westminster became the sovereign's primary residence and seat of government. After fires in 1512 and 1834, the only surviving structures of the medieval palace are Westminster Hall, parts of St Stephen's Chapel, and Jewel Tower.

Jewel Tower was constructed to protect Edward III's personal valuables (the Privy Wardrobe). Detached from other buildings for security and safety, it was incorporated into the palace's precinct walls on the property's southwestern corner. At the time of its construction (1365-1366) the tower was crenelated (had battlements built atop its walls) and protected by a moat on two sides.

DESCRIPTION Jewel Tower is a small three-storey stone tower built in an L-shape. It is partly surrounded by a moat that channelled the River Tyburn to the River Thames. Walls of Westminster Palace once extended east and north from the tower along the moat. The walled area to its northeast was the palace garden. From this area, now a lawn, visitors enter the tower's ground floor and, via a circular stone staircase, its two upper floors.

In the larger of the ground floor's chambers is an English Heritage shop. The chamber's ceiling retains an impressive original ribbed-vault design. In the 14th century, the room contained the office of the Keeper of the Privy Wardrobe. A clerk worked on the floor above, keeping the Wardrobe's records of valuables bought, sold, stored and transferred.

The top floor was the tower's stronghold where, behind an entrance once barred by double doors, the Wardrobe's yeoman guarded the king's personal treasure. Today this floor displays items recovered from the post-Second World War excavation of the palace moat. The collection's highlight is the Palace of Westminster Sword. Discovered in 1948 south of the House of Lords, the 30-inch-long sword was made using pattern welding in the Rhineland c. AD 800. At the time, the Rhineland was the political centre of Charlemagne's empire.

VISITOR INFO 🌣 *Apr-Oct* 10am-5pm daily, *Nov-Mar* 10am-4pm *Sa, Su* Closed 1 *Jan*, 24-26 *Dec* 💷 Adult £4.20, Child (5-15y) £2.50, Concession £3.80, Group Discount 15% discount for 11+. English Heritage Members Free 🅕 Shop. Toilets are at Westminster station. 🍽 The Crown Jewels were never stored at Jewel Tower. Instead they were kept at Westminster Abbey (from 1042 until they were stolen in 1303), and at the Tower of London (from their recovery in 1303 onward).

CITY WALL (NORTHWESTERN REMAINS)
London EC2

HISTORY Unlike most other cities in Britain or elsewhere in the Roman Empire, Roman London (Londinium) evolved from neither a pre-Roman settlement nor a former Roman military base. Instead, it started c. AD 47 as a commercial hub.

Lacking fortifications, around AD 60 this early London was captured by the Iceni Queen Boudica and her followers. They then burnt it to the ground and massacred its inhabitants.

In AD 120, about the time of Emperor Hadrian toured the province, an 11-acre (4.5 hectare) rectangular stone fort was built in the city's northeast. Because the city had become the provincial capital after Boudica's revolt, the fort was garrisoned by the provincial governor's household troops: 1,000 men from Britannia's three legions and its auxiliary cavalry regiments.

Around AD 200, the fort's outer walls were incorporated into a two-mile stone wall built on the city's landward side. A one-mile-long riverside wall was then built in stages between AD 240 and 360 to protect the city from increasing Saxon raids. Although its design was similar to the landward wall, it was less precisely constructed, and used stone blocks cannibalised from older sacred and military monuments. At about the time the riverside wall was completed, the west gate of the Roman fort was blocked and a new gate built at Aldersgate. Also in the mid-4th century, the eastern landward wall was reinforced with 22 D-shaped towers in a new design used throughout the Western and Eastern Roman Empires. Each tower was 26-30 feet tall with a platform for a catapult.

The last work on the city's defences was at the end of the century when the wall's southeastern corner, now the location of the Tower of London, was reinforced. We are not aware of any construction or repairs to the wall after Roman troops left Britain to defend Italy c. AD 407.

As Saxon attacks increased, Roman Britain submerged into the Dark Ages and the city disappeared from historical view. The last we read of Londinium is when Romano-Britains flee there after being defeated by Saxons at the Battle of Crayford (AD 457). Some historians call this period of collapse Sub-Roman Britain. [Continued in the next entry: CITY WALL (SOUTHEASTERN REMAINS).]

DESCRIPTION Of the two-mile-long landward city wall, only a few hundred feet still exist. Remains are concentrated in two areas of the City: northwest near the Barbican, and southeast at the Tower of London. The key sections of wall in the northwest are described below.

Roman Remains. In the garden along Noble Street is the base of the Roman fort's western wall. At its southern-most point is the base of one of its internal turrets that once allowed access to the sentry walk. When the fort was subsumed by the new city wall c. AD 200, a wall was built from this point west to modern-day Ludgate Circus then south to the River Thames. At the same time the fort wall was thickened. This more recent Roman work survives to a height of 8 feet (2.4 m). Under the Museum of London to its north is a tower of the fort's western gate. Entry is restricted to Museum of London tours.

Medieval Remains. A mix of medieval building techniques can be seen in the garden to the west of Noble Street on top of the original Roman wall's ruins. Following the line of the wall north over the road named London Wall are more substantial remains: 13th century circular bastions (tower-like defences).

The first of the bastions was built to a height of three stories during the reign of Henry III. Arrow slits are still visible as are sockets used for scaffolding during construction. To the north in the garden next to the Barber-Surgeons Guild Hall is the second bastion. In 1607 it was built into the western end of the guild's courtroom. The courtroom was destroyed in the Great Fire of 1666, rebuilt, and then destroyed by the Blitz (bombing) in 1940. From the northern-most point in the garden east of the Museum of London, visitors can seen the third bastion at the northwestern corner of the Roman fort and city wall.

East from the corner is the base of the remaining 13th century bastion, and a much higher section of wall. The best vantage point here is opposite the

Church of St Giles Without Cripplegate now on Barbican Estate. Access is from Wood Street to the east.

The only surviving section of the wall with crenelations (battlements) is in St Alphage's Gardens. These brick battlements date from 1477 when the Mayor of London ordered the repair of the city walls during the Wars of the Roses (1455-1487). The area is under redevelopment but access is expected to be from Fore Street to the north and London Wall to the south.

VISITOR INFO 🌐 24 hours daily 💲 Free ⓕ Facilities at Museum of London.

CITY WALL (SOUTHEASTERN REMAINS)
London EC3

HISTORY [Continued from the previous entry.] Two centuries after the Roman legions departed, a Saxon settlement - Lundenwic (London port) - grew on the Strand a mile west of abandoned Londinium. In the mid-9th century the unfortified settlement was attacked again and again by Vikings until the Saxon king, Alfred the Great, led his people from the Strand to Lundenburgh (London fort) and the protection of its ancient Roman city walls. The Saxons then built a defensive South-Werk on an island on the southern bank of the River Thames. The South-Werk protected a ferry crossing between Lundenburgh and the island (now Southwark). Both South-Werk and Lundenburgh were on the front line of Alfred's system of defensive burghs.

London's city walls proved their effectiveness in withstanding renewed assaults by Vikings, and even by the (Viking-descended) Normans in 1066. When the city reached an agreement with the Normans in the weeks after William the Conqueror's victory over the Saxon king Harold II, the victors constructed three wooden castles within its walls to control London. Two castles were on the city's western side: Montfichet's Tower near Ludgate, and Baynard Castle south of Montfichet's on the River Thames. The other castle was on the city's eastern side. While all three were rebuilt in stone, the only castle to survive beyond the medieval period was the one in the east, the Tower of London.

Like Montfichet's Tower and Baynard Castle, the Roman riverside city wall failed to survive beyond the medieval period. It disappeared by the end of the 12th century. While there is no record of attempts to stall its disappearance, we do know of medieval work to improve the landward wall and its gates.

During the reigns of John I and Henry III, hollow rubble-built bastions were added to the wall in the west and north. Under Henry's successor, Edward I, extra defensive works were built outside Cripplegate, previously the northern gate of a Roman fort. Those works came to be called the Barbican, meaning fortified outpost or gateway, and still give their name to the area.

To the south, Edward allowed the Dominican Friars (Blackfriars) to move from Holborn to the Thameside area still named for them. As part of the move in the 1270s, he had them remove the city wall between the River Thames and Ludgate and rebuild it to the west around their precinct along the Fleet River.

In 1415 the postern to the Moorfields north of London was replaced by Moorgate. In the 1760s, it and all other city gates were demolished to improve traffic flow. At the time, the city wall was rapidly disappearing due to its demolition for building materials and its incorporation into adjacent buildings. The wall only reappeared after the Second World War when sections of it were among the highest structures still standing in bomb-ravaged London.

Besides these remains, the wall has had a lasting impact on the names of city localities and thoroughfares: London Wall, Ludgate, Newgate, Aldersgate, Cripplegate, Bishopsgate, Aldgate, Barbican and Houndsditch. Historically, the city wall defined the shape of London until the 16th century. Today, it helps define the boundaries of the municipality known as the City of London.

DESCRIPTION Significant sections of wall in the southeast are described below.

Roman Remains. In the public courtyard of the Grange City Hotel (8-10 Cooper's Row, London EC3N 2BQ), the Roman wall can be seen to the original height of the Roman sentry walk, 14.4 feet (4.4 m). A similar stretch of wall is next to the north end of Tower Hill pedestrian underpass. Next to it is a replica of the tombstone inscription of Julius Classicianus, the provincial treasurer appointed by the Roman Emperor Nero (AD 15-68) after of Boudica's revolt. In front of the wall is a statue of Roman Emperor Trajan (AD 53-117).

Inside the Tower of London, D-shaped 4th century Roman foundations of Wardrobe Tower can be seen as can the outline of the Roman landward wall. The outline includes that of a small internal 3rd century turret east of the White Tower at the point the wall changes direction.

A second section of Roman wall within the Tower is of the riverside wall that once ran from southeast of the White Tower to Blackfriars. It can be seen south of the White Tower opposite the Ravens Shop.

Medieval Remains. The wall's first significant medieval piece of wall is in the public courtyard of the Grange City Hotel. It survives to 35 feet (10.6 m). During the medieval period it was heightened by 21 feet (6.2 m), work evident in its irregular masonry. Other medieval features include a double staircase to the sentry walk in the middle of this stretch of wall, archer's loopholes either side of the staircase, and socket holes for a wooden walkway.

A similar section is next to the northern end of Tower Hill pedestrian underpass. It was heightened and repaired as shown by the medieval stonework with the sentry walk narrowed to 3 feet (0.9 m).

The final piece of medieval city wall is the remains of a multi-angular tower for a postern on Tower Hill. Built before 1190, it was rebuilt by Henry III or his son Edward I during their expansions of the Tower of London. Arrow slits in the tower, the groove of the portcullis, the doorway to the guardroom, and the base of the staircase can be seen between the southern end of the pedestrian underpass and the Tower's northern moat.

VISITOR INFO 🕐 24 hours daily 🅿 Free 🛈 Toilets are inside the Tower of London and outside near its Welcome Centre. Refreshments range from those on Tower Wharf to the Grange City Hotel. 🖼 A model of Roman London is in the crypt of All Hallows by the Tower (Byward Street, London EC3R 5BJ) just to the west of the Tower of London. It also has artifacts from Roman times onward.

The nearest city walls to London's are those of St Albans 20 miles north-northwest. A two-mile-long wall was built to protect Verulamium (St Albans) between AD 265 and 270. Remains of its London Gate are still impressive.

MI6 HEADQUARTERS
85 Albert Embankment, London SE1 7TP

HISTORY MI6, officially the Secret Intelligence Service (SIS), gathers foreign intelligence for the British government. It is Britain's equivalent of the CIA.

SIS traces its lineage to the Secret Service Bureau (SSB). Established in 1909, the SSB was a joint-venture of the Admiralty (Navy) and War Office (Army). By the First World War, the Navy's contribution to the venture had specialized in foreign intelligence, the Army's in domestic counter-intelligence. In 1916, the Army's section was renamed Military Intelligence 5 (MI5), the Navy's Military Intelligence 6 (MI6). Although their official names have changed over the years, they are still known by their abbreviations, MI5 and MI6.

During the Second World War and the Cold War, MI5 and MI6 were penetrated by the Soviet Union using British double agents. Of the British agents, Kim Philby's treason was the most damaging. Recruited in Austria during the 1930s by Communist activist Litzi Friedmann, Philby's betrayal led to the murder of thousands of men and women before he defected in 1961.

From this low point, MI6 performance against the Soviet bloc improved through the 1960s until the dissolution of the Soviet Union in 1991. The same period saw the rise of MI6's most famous fictional spy, Commander James Bond (Agent 007), in a series of movies starting with *Dr. No* (1962).

DESCRIPTION MI6's headquarters is a futuristic, specially-built structure next to the River Thames in Vauxhall. Approved by the government in 1987, it was operational in 1995. As an intelligence service fortress in the heart of London, it features defenses against bombs and rockets, electronic espionage, and attacks on the building's external services such as its power supply.

The headquarters' defences proved effective in September 2000 when it was attacked by the Real IRA using a Soviet-made RPG-22 anti-tank rocket. Although its eight floor was hit, damage was only superficial.

The headquarters was also hit with a bomb blast in the opening sequence of the James Bond movie *The World is Not Enough* (1999). It was the first time filming was allowed inside the building.

VISITOR INFO 🌐 24-hours daily (outside only) 💷 Free 🚻 None 🅿️ Located on the Thames's other side in Millbank is MI5's headquarters, Thames House.

TOWER OF LONDON
London EC3N 4AB
+44 (0)20 3166 6000   ★   hrp.org.uk/TowerOfLondon

HISTORY Initiated by William the Conqueror (William I of England), this royal fortress incorporates parts of London's Roman city walls, and architectural influences of Norman castles in France, of Crusader castles in the Middle East, and of late medieval firearms technology. Reinforced over the centuries by William's successors, the Tower is the most famous and well-preserved medieval fortification in Europe.

Seven kings above all are responsible for the Tower of London's layout. William I chose the site in 1066 so his temporary motte-and-bailey castle would be buttressed by the Roman landward city wall to the east and riverside city wall to the south. He commenced, and his son William II completed, the stone keep (the White Tower) and a circuit of stone walls encircling it.

In the 1190s under Richard I, the castle was extended north and west along the River Thames to make an outer bailey (now the Inner Ward). The Bell Tower, still the western-most point on the Inner Wall, dates from this period.

Immediately following Richard's successor, John I, were two kings who transformed the Tower into a truly great fortress: Henry III and his son Edward I. In his near-half-century reign (1216-1272), Henry reinforced the inner bailey wall (now the Inmost Walls and Ward), extended the outer bailey east and north (Inner Ward and Walls), and created a new watergate (part of Bloody Tower).

Edward I completed his father's building works and started an even greater construction programme in the 1270s. He encircled Henry's outer walls with another circuit of curtain walls to create a new outer bailey, the Outer Ward. This concentric castle's defences were in turn surrounded by a deep moat.

But it is to the Tower's south and southwest that Edward's engineering feats were most impressive. He reclaimed land from the Thames (now Water Lane), converted the existing watergate into a tower controlling access to the Inner Ward (Bloody Tower), and rearranged land gates so entry to the Outer Ward was via drawbridges and gates of three new towers to the southwest: Lion, Middle, and Byward Towers. In the 14th century Edward I's son and grandson, Edward II and III, continued to reinforce the riverside Outer Wall, and to extend Tower Wharf from next to Lion Tower along the entire riverside curtain wall.

By this time kings and their allies had used the Tower as a refuge on more than half a dozen occasions. In 1141, Londoners blockaded the Tower until the Constable of the Tower changed sides from supporting the claim to the throne of Empress Matilda, daughter of Henry I, to supporting that of Henry's nephew Stephen. Half a century later, Richard I's regent, the Bishop of Ely, was besieged in the Tower by Prince John, rebel barons and Londoners.

After John became king, he was besieged at the Tower in 1215 by rebel barons and Londoners led by the Constable of the city's western riverside fortress, Baynard's Castle. In the end, John granted the Magna Carta and gave up the fortress as a pledge that he would honour it. The following year, some of the barons invited Prince Louis, the son of the French king Philip II, to England. For a year and a half the Tower was a French base until Louis' forces were defeated at Lincoln (May 1217) and Dover (August 1217) by those of John's successor, Henry III.

Like John, Henry III was also in regular conflict with his barons. Similarly he sought refuge at the Tower in 1236, 1238 and 1263. Four years later, still during his reign, the Earl of Gloucester led a new revolt supported by Londoners and besieged the Papal Legate in the Tower.

The following century witnessed the Tower's most famous capture, that of 1381 during the Peasants Revolt. Richard II had left the fortress to negotiate when a party of rebels gained entry to the fortress. After dragging several of the king's ministers from sanctuary in the chapel, the rebels beheaded them on

Tower Hill. Richard II sheltered at the Tower again in 1387 when the barons clashed with his favourite, the Earl of Oxford.

During Jack Cade's rebellion in 1450, rebels besieged the Tower until the Lord Treasurer was handed over for trial and execution. Five years later during the Wars of the Roses between the Houses of Lancaster and York, the Tower was besieged twice.

On the first occasion, 1460, it was held by Lancastrians. Yorkists occupied London and supported by Londoners blockaded the Tower. Gunfire was then exchanged between the Tower and the City. The Lancastrians surrendered the Tower only after their army was defeated at the Battle of Northampton.

On the second occasion, 1471, the Tower was held by Yorkists. After the Lancastrians were refused entry to the City and had been defeated at the Battle of Barnet 11 miles north-northwest of London, the Vice Admiral of the Lancastrian fleet laid siege to the City and Tower. The Lancastrians bombarded London for several days until, unable to breach its defences, they withdrew.

The last time the Tower's garrison attacked hostile forces was in 1554 when its gunners fired on Sir Thomas Wyatt's rebels during Wyatt's Rebellion. (The unsuccessful uprising had been sparked by Mary I's decision to marry the future Philip II of Spain.) The castle was last attacked during the Second World War when bombs destroyed its Northern Bastion.

DESCRIPTION The Tower of London is a commanding medieval castle set on the eastern edge of the City. Outwards from the centre its defences are the Keep, Inmost Walls, Inner Walls, Outer Walls, Moat, and Tower outside the Moat.

Keep. At the core of the castle's defences is the keep, the White Tower, its last line of defence and oldest medieval structure. Constructed 1078-1097, this immense rectangular building is impressive even by modern standards with a height of 90 feet (27.5 m), and walls up to 13 feet (4 m) thick. While the Saxons were unused to such engineering feats and could reasonably be expected to be intimidated by it, the Normans were practiced castle builders having constructed keeps of a similar design in Normandy since the 10th century.

Inmost Walls. Little is known of the original Norman castle erected in 1067. However, we do know it was roughly rectangular with outer defences of the landward Roman city wall on the east, riverside Roman city wall on the south, and a ditch and wooden palisade on the west and north.

Just as its original wooden tower was replaced by the White Tower, the wooden palisades were replaced by a stone wall that defined the castle's western and northern perimeter for a century afterwards. At the ward's northeastern corner we have remains of Wardrobe Tower, built during the 1160s or 1170s. At the other three corners are the remains of Coldharbour Gate (northwestern), Wakefield Tower (southwestern), and Lanthorn Tower (southeastern). The latter two date from the 1220s, the former from the 1230s.

Inner Walls. The Inner Walls reflect the location of the castle's outer defences at the end of Henry III's reign (1272). The oldest part of these defences is Bell Tower at the circuit's southwestern corner and the southern wall extending east. Both date from the 1190s during the reign of Richard I.

Except for the wall between Wakefield and Lanthorn Towers (common to both the Inmost Ward and the Inner Ward), the rest of the southern, eastern and northern walls are the result of Henry III's ambitious building programme. From the 1240s this programme expanded the castle to the north (wall reinforced by Brick, Bowyer, Flint, Devereux Towers) and, for the first time, beyond the Roman city walls to the east (Salt, Broad Arrow, Constable, Martin Towers).

Henry III's son, Edward I, completed the remaining walls and towers. Edward made Henry's watergate into the main entrance to the inner ward, incorporating it into what became known as Bloody Tower. The existing city entrance was replaced with a western wall between Henry III's Devereux Tower in the north and Richard I's Bell Tower in the south. Edward reinforced this wall with the new Beauchamp Tower half way along it.

Today the Inner Walls enclose buildings ranging in age from the 16th century's Queen's House and Chapel Royal of St Peter ad Vincula (Latin for "St Peter in Chains") to the mid-19th century Officers Mess and Waterloo Barracks. The Barracks, also known as the Jewel House, now stores the Crown Jewels. Sentries from the Tower Guard stand outside the Jewel House and the Queens' House. The Queen's House, built during the reign of Henry VIII, was intended as the residence for the Lieutenant of the Tower. It fulfills the same purpose today as the Resident Governor's accommodation. Situated between the Queen's House and the Chapel Royal are Tower Green and the scaffold site, the scene of many beheadings the most infamous of which occurred on Henry's orders.

Outer Walls. The Outer Walls reflect the location of the castle's outer defences at the end of Edward I's reign (1307). Returning from the Ninth Crusade in 1274, Edward set about converting the fortress into a modern concentric castle. He built a second set of curtain walls outside those of his father, walls that extended the castle to the west, north, east and – by reclaiming land from the Thames – to the south. Also to the south he built a new watergate, protected by St Thomas's Tower, later known as Traitor's Gate.

As part of the new city entrance, Byward Tower was constructed in the southwestern corner of a new (outer) curtain wall. This tower, two rounded towers at the new wall's northern corners (Legge's Mount in the northwest, and Brass Mount in the northeast), Devlin Tower at its southeastern corner, and Well Tower west of Devlin Tower reinforced the outer wall.

Reigns of Edward II (1307-1327) and Edward III (1327-1377) saw further development of the outer wall with the crenelation of the southern wall from St Thomas's Tower to Develin Tower, and a new tower with a small watergate, Cradle Tower, inset in this section of wall. The northern end of the eastern wall was augmented by two rectangular projections, likely for catapults.

The last major defensive enhancements to the fortress were five centuries later, in the mid-19th century. Enhancements included constructing shell-proof casemates (fortified gun emplacements) in the east and west, improvements in walls for artillery and riflery in the west and north, and the addition of the North Bastion with four tiers of guns at the wall's most northerly point. With the exception of the North Bastion (destroyed by a bomb in 1940) all these features survive today.

Moat. A defensive ditch existed outside the Roman city walls from the 3rd century and surrounded the original Norman castle since the 11th. As the castle expanded so did the ditch until it evolved into a water-filled moat in its current location as part of Edward I's defences.

In the centuries that followed it proved difficult to maintain the moat despite efforts including the retaining wall built from 1670 to 1683 and still visible today. Its declining effectiveness and an increasing concern for sanitation led to its draining in 1843. For the most part, the moat retains its original dimensions including a width of up to 160 feet (50 m).

Tower outside the Moat. The most prominent part of the Tower outside the Moat is Middle Tower, a twin-towered gatehouse at the moat's southwestern extremity. Like the Outer Walls, it was built by Edward I as a defensive layer in his concentric castle. It was positioned as its name implies between the Byward Tower and the since-demolished semi-circular Lion Tower. Lion Tower was the castle's barbican, comprising two gates and a drawbridge. Remains of its draw-bridge pit and outer wall can be seen northwest of Middle Tower.

Lion, Middle and Byward Towers together constituted the Tower's rein-forced city entrance. Each had a portcullis, a gate and drawbridge. Middle and Byward Towers, connected over the moat by a causeway that replaced the original drawbridge, remain the main public entrance to the Tower. Another public entrance for groups with pre-booked tickets, and a general public exit, is east of St Thomas's Tower on Tower Wharf.

VISITOR INFO 🏰 *Mar-Oct* 10am-5.30pm *Su-Mo,* 9am-5.30pm *Tu-Sa.* **Nov-Feb** 10am-4.30pm *Su-Mo,* 9am-4.30pm *Tu-Sa.* Closed 1 *Jan* and 24-26 *Dec.* 🎫 Adult £24.50, Child (5-15y) £11.00, Concession £18.70, Family (2 adults, 3 children) £60.70. Tickets can be bought from the Tower's website at a discount to the above prices. ℹ️ Wide range of facilities: guidebooks, disabled access, toilets, café, shops, childrens' activities, education, tours, events, Holy Communion. 🐾 The Tower was associated with exotic animals for centuries. Henry III established the Menagerie (Zoo) when given an elephant by Louis IX of France, leopards by Emperor Frederick II, and a polar bear by Haakon IV of Norway. The number of animals grew and over time some gave their name to parts of the castle such as Lion Tower. In 1835 the animals were given to London Zoo.

Castles and former castles in or near London (listed by distance from the Tower of London) are Eltham Palace (7 miles southeast), Eynsford Castle (16 miles southeast), Windsor Castle (25 miles west), St Leonard's Tower (26 miles southeast), Rochester Castle (26 miles east-southeast), and Berkhamsted Castle (27 miles northwest). All the fortifications were initiated in Norman times.

Of the six, Windsor Castle is most similar to the Tower of London. Built by William the Conqueror as a earth-and-wood motte-and-bailey castle soon after 1066, it was later rebuilt in stone. It was enlarged over the centuries by some of the same kings responsible for the Tower's expansions: Henry III and Edward III. Unlike the Tower, Windsor Castle is today a royal residence.

Berkhamsted Castle also started as a motte-and-bailey base for William the Conqueror in 1066. Although he defeated and killed the Saxon king Harold II Godwinson at the Battle of Hastings (14 October), in London the Witenagemot (a Saxon parliament comprised of the kingdom's key nobles) elected Edgar the Ætheling as England's king. Edgar's troops were defeated at Southwark but held London Bridge against the Normans. William then marched his army east along the Thames then north to Berkhamsted. In December Saxon resistance crumbled, London surrendered, and William was crowned king at Westminster Abbey on Christmas Day. By that time the building of the Tower of London has started.

Key to Fortifications – Tower of London

Keep

Tower
1 White *

Inmost Walls and Inmost Ward

Towers
2 Coldharbour Gate (remains)
3 Wardrobe (remains)
4 Wakefield
5 Lanthorn

Other
a Roman landward city wall (site)
b Roman riverside city wall (remains)
c Great Hall (site)
d Raven Aviary

Inner Walls and Inner Ward

Towers
4 Wakefield *
5 Lanthorn *
6 Salt *
7 Broad Arrow *
8 Constable *
9 Martin *
10 Brick
11 Bowyer
12 Flint
13 Devereux
14 Beauchamp *
15 Bell
16 Bloody *

Other
e Queen's House
f Tower Green
g Scaffold (site)
h Chapel Royal of St Peter ad Vincula*
i Waterloo Barracks and Jewel House *
j Officers Mess and Fusiliers Museum *
k New Armouries *

Outer Walls and Outer Ward

Towers
17 Byward
18 St Thomas's *
19 Cradle *
20 Well
21 Develin
22 Brass Mount
23 Legge's Mount

Other
l Water Lane
m Mint Lane

Moat

Towers
24 Barbican (site)
25 North Bastion (site)

Other
n Moat
o Tennis court

Tower outside the Moat

Towers
26 Middle
27 Lion (remains)

Other
p Tower Bridge Road
q Alternate entrance for groups with
   pre-booked tickets and public exit
r Tower Wharf
s Ferry Wharf
t Main public entrance and exit
u Welcome Centre
v Ticket Office
w Tower Hill Road
x Tower Hill
y City Walls, Tower Hill Underground
   underpass and Postern Gate (remains)

* indicates towers and buildings open to visitors

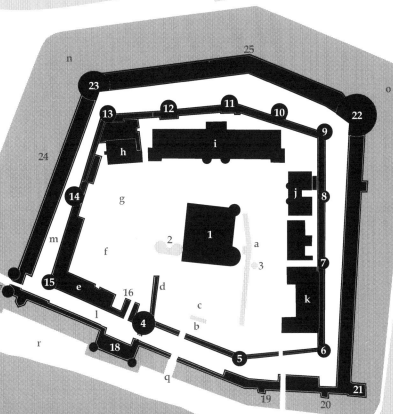

Fortifications
Tower of London

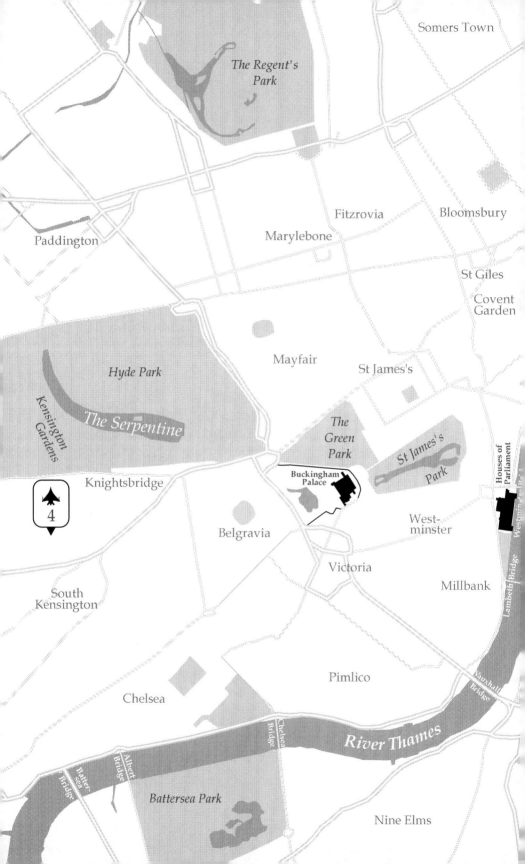

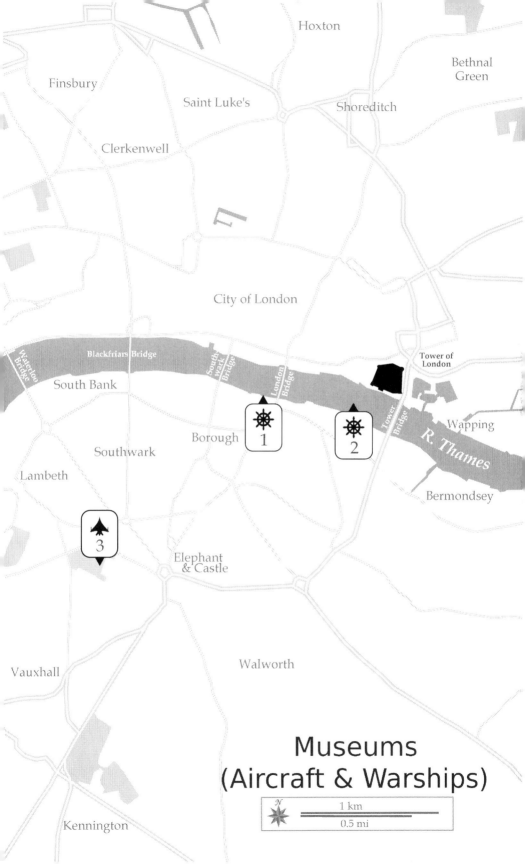

Hoxton

Bethnal
Green

Finsbury

Saint Luke's

Shoreditch

Clerkenwell

City of London

Waterloo Bridge

Blackfriars Bridge

South
wark
Bridge

London
Bridge

Tower of
London

South Bank

Tower Bridge

Wapping

1

2

R. Thames

Borough

Southwark

Lambeth

Bermondsey

3

Elephant
& Castle

Walworth

Vauxhall

Museums
(Aircraft & Warships)

N

1 km

0.5 mi

Kennington

Museums (Aircraft & Warships)

Golden Hinde II
St Mary Overie Dock, Cathedral Street, London SE1 9DE
+44 (0)20 7403 0123   ★   goldenhinde.co.uk

HISTORY *Golden Hinde II* is the recreation of an Elizabethan galleon captained by Francis Drake. The original *Golden Hinde* was the second ship (Drake the first captain) to circumnavigate the globe. (Magellan, captain of the Spanish carrack *Victoria* – the first ship to circle the Earth – was killed in 1522 travelling through the Philippine Archipelago during his historic journey).

Commissioned by Queen Elizabeth I in 1577, *Golden Hinde* sailed from Plymouth to the South Atlantic and around the southern tip of South America through Magellan Strait into the Pacific Ocean. There the ship sailed north along the South American coast, raided the Spanish port of Valparaiso (1578) and captured treasure-laden Spanish ships. After continuing past Spain's northern-most territorial claim at Point Loma near modern-day San Diego, California, Drake went ashore, held Communion, and claimed the land for England (1579).

Golden Hinde then sailed across the Pacific, through the Indonesian Archi-pelago, across the Indian Ocean, around Africa's Cape of Good Hope, and north to Plymouth (1580). Drake was knighted by Elizabeth the next year.

Early in the Anglo-Spanish War (1585-1604), Drake led a fleet that raided Spain, and Spanish colonies in Florida, the Caribbean, and South America. In 1587 he destroyed 100 Spanish ships in and around Cadiz, and the next year was deputy commander of the fleet that defeated the Spanish Armada.

DESCRIPTION This "living history" museum is a window into life aboard a 16th century warship. Accommodation on this small (120 feet long, 20 feet wide) three-masted vessel ranges from Drake's spacious cabin on the Half Deck, through the officers' cramped but well-lit quarters in the Armoury below, to the dark and creaking Gun Deck shared by 40 men and 14 cannons (12 four-pounder Minions, 2-pounder Falcons). Other cannons are on the fo'c'sle (contraction of forecastle) at the front of the ship, and aft (aftercastle) at the vessel's rear.

As their names suggest, the fo'c'sle and aft were originally raised fighting platforms. From the open decks atop these "castles", archers and - from the 15th century - swivel guns were used to clear the decks of enemy ships prior to boarding them or to disrupt enemy boarding parties.

VISITOR INFO 🕙 10am-5.30pm daily 💷 Self-guided tour: Adult £6, Child and Concession £4.50, Family £18 ℹ️ No facilities 🧭 200 yards west of the *Golden Hinde* on Southbank is another Elizabethan recreation, the Globe Theatre. A faithful reconstruction of William Shakespeare's open-air playhouse, the Globe hosts his plays from April to October each year (shakespearesglobe.com).

HMS Belfast
The Queen's Walk, London SE1 2JH
+44 (0)20 7940 6300 ★ hmsbelfast.iwm.org.uk

HISTORY *Belfast* is Europe's last big-gun warship of the Second World War.

Following the First World War, politicians put their faith in the League of Nations and international treaties to prevent future wars. Agreements to freeze the naval status quo included the Washington Treaty (1922), and the London Naval Agreement (1930) restricting capital ships' tonnage.

Japan's *Mogami*-class cruisers (launched 1931-1937) kept to the letter of the agreements with a displacement of only 8,500 tonnes. However their 15 6.1-inch guns outclassed equivalent ships in rival navies and upset the status quo.

Town-class light cruisers (launched 1934-1939) were Britain's answer to the *Mogami*. *Belfast*, a *Town*-class variant, was commissioned on 5 August 1939. On the outbreak of war, she patrolled the North Sea until hitting a mine on 21 November. The damage took her out of action for three years.

In November 1942 *Belfast* rejoined the Home Fleet. 1943 saw her awarded two battle honours: "Arctic" for defending Allied convoys, and "North Cape". The latter was won off northern Norway in the last big-gun engagement between capital ships in European waters. *Belfast* was the first British ship to make radar contact with battlecruiser *Scharnhorst*. She then took part throughout the 11-hour battle that ended with the sinking of the German warship.

Belfast's final battle honour of the war, "Normandy", was awarded for her shore bombardment supporting the D-Day landings (6 June 1944) and the Allied push inland. In 1945 she was assigned to the British Pacific Fleet.

Despite arriving too late to see action, the Far East was *Belfast*'s primary operating area until her decommissioning. It was also where she was awarded a final battle honour, "Korea", for service in the Korean War (1950-1953).

Decommissioned in 1963, *Belfast* was saved from the scrapyard through efforts of her former crew. In 1971 she was towed from Portsmouth to London and opened to the public on Trafalgar Day.

DESCRIPTION This mighty cruiser, 613 feet-long and 69 feet-wide at its beam, has nine decks open to visitors. An audio tour (included with admission) starts on the quarterdeck and Y Turret (a battery of three 6-inch guns) at the aft of the ship. Upon entering *Belfast* and passing its chapel, a ladder leads down to the Boiler and Engine Rooms. Here visitors can see machinery including four steam turbines that once propelled the ship at up to 32 knots (36mph/58kph).

Back up on the main exhibition deck past the galley, medical facilities and stores are exhibitions "HMS *Belfast* in War and Peace" and "Life at Sea". Forward of the exhibitions is the Arctic Messdeck where some of the ship's 750-man crew were quartered. A ladder near the mess deck leads down to the 6-inch Shell Room and Magazine that once fed B Turret (another battery with three 6-inch guns). In total, *Belfast* has four of these turrets.

The tour then proceeds up ladders to the fo'c'sle on the upper deck, and from there up into the bridge superstructure, the command and operations heart of the ship: Admiral's Bridge, Electronic Warfare Office, Gun Direction Platform, Compass Platform and Operations Room.

After descending through the bridge superstructure, the tour passes two batteries of twin 4-inch HA/LA (High Angle/Low Angle) dual-purpose guns. From there, the tour returns to the quarterdeck where it concludes.

VISITOR INFO ☀ *Mar-Oct* 10am-6pm daily; *Nov-Feb* 10am-5pm daily. Closed 24-26 *Dec* 🄬 Adult £14.50, Child (5-15y) £7.25, Concession £11.60 🅕 Restrooms, audio guides, café, shop. Much of the ship is inaccessible to wheelchairs.

IMPERIAL WAR MUSEUM LONDON
Lambeth Road, London SE1 6HZ
+44 (0)20 7416 5000   ★   iwm.org.uk/visits/iwm-london

HISTORY This is Britain's national military museum of wars involving British and Commonwealth forces from the First World War (1914-1918) onward.

The importance of the First World War in the history of warfare was recognised at the time. In 1917, the British Cabinet decided to create a national war museum to chronicle the war in objects used to fight it. An Act of Parliament in 1920 established the Imperial War Museum to present not just Britain's role but that of its Dominions: Australia, Canada, New Zealand, Rhodesia and South Africa. After being housed in Crystal Palace and South Kensington, it opened in its current building (formerly Bethlehem Royal Hospital, dating from 1814).

The museum's scope was widened after 1945 to include the Second World War with its coverage extended again in 1953 to cover all military operations involving Britain or the Commonwealth since the outbreak of the First World War. Over more than half a century since then, British and Commonwealth Forces have been involved in dozens of operations on most continents. The museum has continued to chronicle their actions.

DESCRIPTION Military hardware is on display well before visitors enter the museum: two 15-inch guns from *Revenge*-class battleships HMS *Ramillies* and HMS *Resolution* embedded in the slope leading up to its main entrance. Inside the museum are five floors devoted to 20th and 21st century military history.

Through the main entrance is "Witnesses to War" featuring large exhibits including a Soviet T34 (in service 1939-1973), German rockets (V-1 and V-2), and British combat aircraft (Supermarine Spitfire Mark 1A and Harrier jump jet). To the rear of the ground floor are the First World War galleries (including a Mk V tank). As well as written information and visual displays explaining the conflict, on display are uniforms, insignia, helmets, weapons, models and dioramas. A similar mix of exhibits is in "Turning Points: 1934-1945" (a first floor gallery mainly focused on the Second World War), and "Peace and Security: 1945-2014" (a second floor gallery bringing the museum's timeline into the 21st century).

In addition to these core galleries are "A Family in Wartime" (first floor, World War Two focus), "Secret War" (second floor, focus on espionage and covert operations actions pitting MI5, MI6, Special Operations Executive and the Special Air Service against Britain's enemies), and on the third floor "Curiosities of War", special exhibitions, and art and photography from museum collections. The fourth and fifth floors contain the Holocaust gallery's entrance and the Lord

Ashcroft Gallery, respectively. The Lord Ashcroft Gallery celebrates Victoria and George Cross recipients, recounting the bravery behind the medals on display.

VISITOR INFO 🌐 10am-6pm daily. Closed 24-26 *Dec* 💷 Free ❶ Restrooms, café, free talks and activities, shops 🔘 During the First English Civil War the museum's site was occupied by a fort that reinforced the southern section of Parliament's earthworks protecting London.

Science Museum
Exhibition Road, South Kensington, London SW7 2DD
+44 (0)87 0870 4868   ★   sciencemuseum.org.uk

HISTORY A world-renowned technology museum, London's Science Museum showcases advances in science and industry over the last 300 years.

The museum has its roots in the Great Exhibition of 1851 held in Hyde Park. Profits from the Exhibition funded the purchase of land south of the park in South Kensington for museums to promote technical education and industry. Items from the Exhibition formed the nucleus of their collections and were temporarily housed at the new Museum of Manufactures. With the opening of South Kensington Museum (1857), the items were transferred there.

In the late 19th century the museum split its science and art collections into the Science Museum and Victoria & Albert Museum (V&A), respectively. In 1928 the Science Museum opened in a new building where it continues today.

DESCRIPTION 15,000 science and technology-related objects are displayed by the museum over seven floors in a quarter-mile-long building. Two of its floors contain items of military interest.

On the ground floor, the "Space" gallery displays life-size replicas of an Indian War Rocket (1790), and a 32lb Rocket on a Congreve Bombarding Frame (1806). A miniature V-2 rocket is in a diorama with a real V-2 in the next gallery, "Making the Modern World". The full-size V-2, captured in 1945, has part of its exterior cut away exposing its engine. In the same gallery is an Avro 504 biplane, the highest production British aircraft in the First World War. These aircraft took part in one of the earliest bombing raids of the war and were also used over London for anti-Zeppelin patrols. On the walkway overlooking the gallery are models of mid-20th century British aircraft.

Many aircraft models are also on the third floor's "Flight" gallery. That gallery also contains two dozen actual aircraft, among them a Fokker E.III (1916) of the First World War, and Hawker Hurricane (1938) and Supermarine Spitfire Mk1a (1940) of the Second. Also from the Second World War is a Messerschmitt Me 163 Komet (1944). With a top speed of 559 mph (900 kmph), the Komet was the only rocket-propelled fighter to see combat. British aircraft from the Jet Age are a Gloster E.28/39 (1941), Hawker P1127 (Harrier jump jet prototype, 1960), and Westland Skeeter Mk12 helicopter (1960).

VISITOR INFO 🌐 10am-6pm daily. Closed 24-26 *Dec* 💷 Free ❶ Full range 🔘
The RAF Museum 8 miles north-northwest also has dozens of aircraft on show.

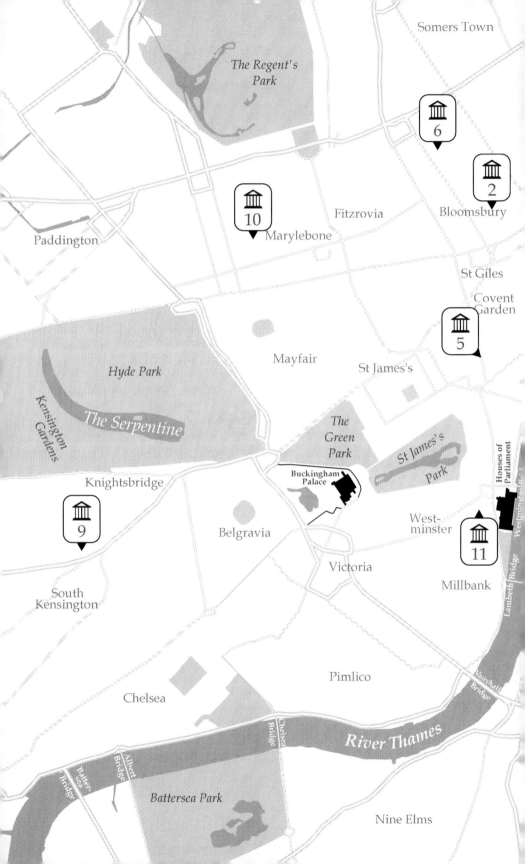

Museums
(General & Sacred)

Museums (General & Sacred)

BANK OF ENGLAND MUSEUM
Bartholomew Lane, London EC2R 8AH
+44 (0)20 7601 5545
bankofengland.co.uk/education/Pages/museum/visiting/default.aspx

HISTORY New Dutch financing techniques combined with the drive of Scottish businessman William Paterson led to the creation of the Bank of England in 1694. That year the bank, as the government's banker and debt manager, sold the first ever bonds issued by a national government. Because the bonds were redeemable in gold, and England was politically stable, investors were satisfied with a lower interest rate than otherwise. Being able to borrow larger sums at the same cost helped England in the War of the Grand Alliance against France, a kingdom with a population and economy three times larger than England's. In wars that followed, the bank had an important role managing the nation's funding needs.

After a small French invasion force landed in northern Wales in 1797, investors nervous about England's progress in the war against Revolutionary France made runs on the bank draining its gold reserves. When the government suspended investors' ability to convert its notes into gold, an Irish Member of Parliament denounced the bank as an "elderly lady in the City of great credit and long standing, who had unfortunately, fallen into bad company". This theme was developed by James Gillray in his famous cartoon "Political Ravishment or The Old Lady of Threadneedle Street in danger!", the origin of the bank's nickname "The Old Lady of Threadneedle Street". While the restriction ended in 1821, gold convertibility was broken again during the First World War, and ended permanently in 1931.

DESCRIPTION A quarter of the museum's displays deal with military and defence matters starting with "The Antwerp Agency". From its foundation, the Bank of England not only raised funds to finance wars but was involved in the distribution of money to the armed forces. Information panels, a print of the siege of Namur (1695), and a book and receipt to Directors of the Bank for money paid to British Army in Flanders (1694-1698) are shown.

From 1793 to 1815 Britain was almost continuously at war with France. Most edged weapons and firearms on display are from this period: a London-manufactured Flintlock musket with a short brass barrel and spring-loaded bayonet (c. 1800), officers' swords, and two prominent wall arrangements in the Rotunda. One of the arrangements consists of pikes, pistols and muskets, the other of the Colours of the Bank of England Volunteer Corps (1798-1814).

After displays on the Bank Piquet (military guard), and First World War is a display on the Second World War with a broader range of artifacts: a helmet marked "BoE HR" (Bank of England Heavy Rescue), fragments of an incendiary bomb (c. 1941), and a £20 note forged by Germany for Operation Bernhard. The display's capstone is a letter from General Dwight Eisenhower, the Supreme Commander of Allied Forces in Europe. The letter thanks the Bank of England for its distribution of money to Allied forces in Europe, a role it first performed at Antwerp in Flanders for William III two and a half centuries before.

VISITOR INFO ❈ 10am-5pm *Mo-Fr.* 10am-1pm Christmas Eve and New Year's Eve. Closed Public and Bank holidays 🅔 Free 🅕 Toilets, shop. Many eateries are open during the week. ⬤ Located at Threadneedle Street since 1734, the bank grew into a large, three-storey island site protected by an imposing windowless curtain wall. Its height and walls give it the appearance of an ornate stone fortress.

BRITISH MUSEUM
Great Russell Street, London WC1B 3DG
+44 (0)20 7323 8000   ★   britishmuseum.org

HISTORY Created by an Act of Parliament in 1753, the British Museum started with three collections. A century of acquisitions forced the museum to move to a new building, and then to move some departments from its new home: Natural History to South Kensington in 1881 (now the Natural History Museum), the library in 1973 (the British Library at St Pancras from 1998).

Today the British Museum is home for some of the world's most important collections of antiquities. Its military artifacts range from a 400,000-year-old Lower Palaeolithic hand axe through arms and armour of ancient Greece and Rome to weapons from Africa.

DESCRIPTION Antiquities are on the Ground, Upper and Lower levels.

Ground Level. Galleries of military interest are Enlightenment Gallery (1), Asia (33-34, 67), Ancient Near East (6-10), and Greece & Rome (12-15, 17-18).

The Enlightenment Gallery (1) is a museum within a museum. Among items housed in the former library named for George III are Neolithic, Bronze and Iron Age axe blades, spear- and arrowheads, and swords and shield bosses from northwestern Europe (4th millennium BC to the 1st century BC); tribal war clubs of stone, wood and whalebone from the Pacific (1st to 19th century AD); Etruscan and Roman arms and armour (7th century BC to 3rd century AD); and European medieval helmets, sword and scabbard, and maces.

Asia galleries contain artifacts from Korea, China, India, Iran and Turkey. The large Gallery 33 focuses mainly on China and on the Indian subcontinent. Highlights are spectacular Indian and Sri Lankan arms: elephant goad, swords and knives (16th to 19th centuries AD), and Chinese arms: bronze swords, halberds, crossbow fittings, and an iron sword in a lacquered scabbard from the Han dynasty (3rd century BC to 2nd century AD).

Of Islamic artifacts (Gallery 34) most notable is the Islamic Arms and Armour display. It covers the arc from Turkey to India with weapons as varied as helmets, shields, maces, scimitars, and a gauntlet sword (15th to 19th century).

Korea is the sole subject of Gallery 67. Its military objects are limited to stone arrowheads from the Neolithic Age (6000-2000 BC), and arrowheads and daggers from the Bronze Age (1000-300 BC) during the Gojoseon Kingdom.

Galleries of the Ancient Near East (6-10) are almost exclusively occupied with stone sculptures (friezes) from the Assyrian Empire. Friezes that decorated palaces portray military campaigns almost 3,000 years ago: river crossings, battle scenes, attacks on enemy towns, a review of prisoners, and triumphal marches.

Greece & Rome galleries on this level focus on ancient Greek civilisations. Mycenaean bronze weapons in Gallery 12 date from around the Siege of Troy (1190 BC). Galleries 13-15 include Corinthian-type bronze helmets, and Persian arrowheads from the Battle of Marathon (490 BC). Stone carvings of Greek infantry and cavalry in the 4th century BC line the walls of Gallery 17, 18 and 21.

Upper Levels. Of interest are Britain & Europe (40, 41, 46, 49, 50, 51), Near East (52, 54, 56, 57), Egypt (64, 65), Japan (93), and Greece & Rome (69-73).

Britain & Europe galleries cover Europe and the Middle East to the end of the Bronze Age (51), Iron Age Europe (50), Roman Britain (49), the Dark Ages (41), Medieval Europe (40), and Early Modern Europe (46). Military treasures are too numerous to list but Gallery 41 "Sutton Hoo and Europe AD 300-1100" is one of many highlights with weapons, parade shield, and helmet and mailcoat from a 7th-century Saxon ship burial.

Ancient Near East galleries feature bronze weapons from Iran (52) and Anatolia and Urartu (54), weapons from the graves of the kings of Ur (56), and a wide variety of Bronze and Iron Age arms from the Levant (57). Flint, bone, wooden and bronze weapons, some dating from not long before the earliest recorded battle at Megiddo (1457 BC), can be seen in Ancient Egypt (64, 65).

Japan (93) has items from the 6th century (iron sword, gilt copper/sliver sword pommel), and the period between the 16th and 19th centuries (composite suit of armour, stirrups, and Samurai swords, daggers and blades).

Five galleries on Greece & Rome have a major military focus. Gallery 69 has displays on Greek Armour, Gladiators, and the Roman Army. A lead bullet for use in a sling is inscribed "feri Pomp." meaning "hit Pomp(eius)". It was made by the socii (Latin for "allies") fighting Roman troops led by Pompeius Strabo (father of Pompey the Great) in the Social War (90-88 BC). Also of note are bronze parade masks and a citizenship document (all early 2nd century AD).

Again focused on Roman arms and armour from both Republican and Imperial periods is Gallery 70. Among dozens of items are an iron sword and tinned bronze scabbard known as "the Sword of Tiberius" (15 BC), bronze military discharge diplomas (AD 79, AD 246), and a suit of parade armour from Egypt made of crocodile-skin (3rd to 4th century AD).

The Etruscan world is the subject of Gallery 71. It starts chronologically with a flint dagger 2800-2400 BC and concludes with the 1st century BC items. Gallery 72 on Ancient Cyprus shows copper, bronze and iron arms and armour, and artwork depicting them from 2300 BC to the 3rd century BC. Greece & Rome's final gallery (73) deals with Greeks in Italy (armour in a corner display).

Lower Level. Relevant galleries are Africa (25), and Greece & Rome (78). In addition to displays of traditional weapons and armour in the Africa gallery (25) - swords, daggers, helmets, arrowheads, chain metal coat, breastplate, shields (palm fibre/cane/hide, hide/silver/leather composites) - is the Throne of Weapons. The chair is comprised mainly of Soviet AK-47 assault rifles.

The final gallery (78) contains ancient Roman stonework inscriptions. One is from AD 194 by Second Legion veterans who had enlisted together in AD 168. Another is a tombstone of a former Imperial bodyguard (2nd century AD).

VISITOR INFO 🌓 10am-5.30pm *Sa-Th*, 10am-8.30pm *Fr* 🄴 Free 🅒 Toilets, cafés, Court Restaurant, shop, luggage store (size smaller than 40x40x50 cm).

GUILDHALL & ART GALLERY
Gresham Street, London EC2V 7HH
+44 (0)20 7332 1313   ★   www.guildhall.cityoflondon.gov.uk
cityoflondon.gov.uk/guildhallartgallery

HISTORY Guildhall has been home to London's municipal government since it was built between 1411 and 1440. Its crypts (dating from the 11th and 12th centuries) and a medieval document (1128) evidence earlier halls on the site.

While Saxon guilds were mainly religious fraternities, Norman guilds had a distinctly commercial character. Each Norman guild had a monopoly on a craft in its town or city. For example, the Armourers guild in London controlled who could make armour in the City. Every craft had an equivalent guild.

Norman kings and their successors recognized the guilds' influence. The French concept of a town governed by a chief magistrate chosen by the town combined with the commercial importance of London's guilds led to a system where the guilds elected one of their members mayor. Just as the king and his royal council met at Westminster, the mayor and his council met at Guildhall.

DESCRIPTION Guildhall has four areas worth seeing: the Great Hall, Guildhall Art Gallery, the Roman Amphitheatre, and the Heritage Gallery.

As the City's only surviving non-religious medieval building, Guildhall features a magnificent Great Hall. Below it are London's largest medieval crypts. Within the Great Hall are civic and military monuments. A stone memorial to Nelson includes a biography and a scene from the Battle of Trafalgar. Elsewhere statues commemorate not only Trafalgar but Nelson's other victories. A memorial to the Duke of Wellington features his statue and a scene from the Battle of Waterloo. Another memorial is to the Royal Fusiliers (City of London Regiment). Crests of Royal Navy ships, British Army regiments, the Royal Marines, and the Royal Air Force decorate the walls.

Nearby is the Guildhall Art Gallery. Of the gallery's artworks on military subjects, most impressive is the massive (18 feet by 25 feet) oil painting by American-born John Copley *The Defeat of the Floating Batteries at Gibraltar*. Commissioned by the Guildhall in 1783, it shows the decisive point in the siege of Gibraltar the previous year when British artillery set fire to French and Spanish floating artillery platforms claimed to be fire-proof.

In the Art Gallery's basement are remains of Roman London's amphitheatre (early 2nd century AD). Apart from its probable use for training soldiers from the neighbouring fort, the amphitheatre's main function was as an arena for gladiators and animals to fight to the death. This entertainment was banned after the triumph of Christianity in the 4th century. The site may have been a meeting place in Saxon times explaining why the earliest guildhall was built upon it.

Also part of Guildhall Art Gallery is the Heritage Gallery. Its temporarily displays are often on military themes or have military aspects.

VISITOR INFO 🌼 10am-5pm *Mo-Sa*, Noon-4pm *Su* 🄵 Free 🄵 Shop, toilets.

MUSEUM OF LONDON
London Wall, London EC2Y 5HN
+44 (0)87 0444 3852   ★   www.museumoflondon.org.uk

HISTORY The Museum of London tells the story of London from prehistoric times to the present day. Although only opened in 1976 it is based on two well-established museums, the Guildhall Museum and the London Museum.

The Guildhall Museum was the world's first local authority museum. Founded in 1826, its main attractions were collections of artifacts from Roman and medieval London discovered over the previous two centuries.

London Museum was founded at Kensington Palace in 1912 partly as a memorial to Edward VII by members of the royal family and nobility. Merged with Guildhall Museum by an Act of Parliament, the resulting Museum of London opened in the Barbican district. It is the world's largest urban museum.

DESCRIPTION A key aspect of the museum's presentation of London's history is its display of weaponry from prehistoric, Roman, Saxon, Viking, late medieval, early modern, Imperial and World War eras in chronological galleries.

Prehistoric objects in the "London before London" gallery range from flint hand axes from as early as 420,000 BC to bronze and iron weapons of the curvilinear design associated with the Celts. "Roman London" covers the period from the Roman invasion of Britain to AD 410. Items from the 1st to 4th century AD include an officer's iron sword and scabbard, iron daggers, catapult bolts, spearheads, bronze and iron shield bosses, and segments of plate and scale armour. Concluding the gallery are artifacts and information on the turmoil of the 3rd century onward as Britain was beset by invaders and imperial usurpers.

"Medieval London" shows evidence from the Thames of the six turbulent centuries from AD 500: Saxon fighting knives (seax/scramasax), shield bosses and spearheads, and Viking swords, many axe heads and long spearheads (some found near old London Bridge, a scene of fighting between Saxons and Vikings).

The next military artifacts are from 1276-1453, a period England was at war with Wales, Scotland and France. As the kingdom's richest city, London's guilds and the Tower of London's arsenal made items shown here: swords, full chainmail shirt and buckler. Towards the end of the medieval gallery is a display of arms and armour covering the period from the 15th and 16th centuries, an era of wars with France as well as the Wars of the Roses (1455-1487). Of note is a two-handed German sword engraved with the imperial eagle of the Holy Roman Empire. Recovered from the Thames near Westminster, it may have been lost by a German soldier accompanying Emperor Charles V's visit to London (1522).

Next is "War, Plague and Fire" (1550s-1660s) with items from the English Civil War: pikeman's armour proof-marked by the Armourers guild (1630-1640), Army suppliers' contracts for Sir Thomas Fairfax's troops (1645), and musketeers' equipment: bandoleer, matchlock musket and powder flask (1630-1640) bearing the arms of the Haberdashers' Company.

On the level below, the "Expanding City" (1670s-1850s) displays flintlock pistols (including four duelling pistols). Nearby, "People's City" (1850s-1940s) has exhibits on the First World War, a movie on the Second World War's Blitz, and examples of incendiary bombs that rained down on London at the time.

VISITOR INFO 🕙 10am-6pm daily. Closed 24-26 *Dec* Ⓔ Free Ⓕ Toilets, cafés, shop, accessible 🚮 The Museum of London Docklands at Canary Wharf in East London also has a number of permanent military-themed exhibits.

NATIONAL PORTRAIT GALLERY
St Martin's Place, London WC2H 0HE
+44 (0)20 7306 0055 ★ npg.org.uk

HISTORY "The history of the world is but the biography of great men" wrote 19th century Scottish historian and philosopher Thomas Carlyle. His era's artistic embodiment of the "great man" approach to history was the National Portrait Gallery. After its establishment in 1856, it was housed in temporary locations until 1896 when its newly designed home opened next to the National Gallery.

DESCRIPTION Of the institution's 42 rooms, four are devoted to military topics while many others feature famous English and British commanders and their foes. The Gallery's earliest subject is on the second floor: Henry VI (1421-1471) in Room 1 "The early Tudors". In the next room (2 "Elizabethan England") are the first non-royal military leaders: Sir Walter Raleigh (1552-1618) and Sir Henry Unton (1558-1596), both veterans of the long-running Anglo-Spanish War.

Other military commanders depicted in the rooms that follow include Civil War generals Oliver Cromwell (1599-1658) and George Monck (1608-1670) (both Room 7 "Charles II"), General John Churchill (1650-1722) who deserted James II for William of Orange in 1688 (8 "The Later Stuarts"), Major General Robert Clive (1725-1774) who established the British foothold in eastern India and General James Wolfe (1727-1759) who captured Quebec (both 14 "Britain becomes a World Power"), Field Marshal Arthur Wellesley, the Duke of Wellington (1769-1852) and Admiral Horatio Nelson (1758-1805) (both 17 "Royalty, Celebrity and Scandal"), and Field Marshal Horatio Kitchener (1850-1916) and the general Kitchener failed to relieve in the Sudan, the legendary General Charles Gordon (1833-1885) (both 23 "Expansion and Empire").

Room 30 "We are making a New World: Britain 1914-18" is of necessity dominated by military leaders with portraits of Field Marshal Jan Smuts (1870-

1950), Admiral John Jellicoe (1859-1935), and Admiral David Beatty (1871-1936). The room also features two very large paintings at either end: *General Officers of World War* I by John Sargent, and *Statesmen of World War I* by Sir James Guthrie. Room 31 "A National Portrait: Britain 1919-59" shows portraits of military theorist Sir Basil Liddell Hart (1895-1970) and Field Marshal Bernard Montgomery (1887-1976).

VISITOR INFO 10am-6pm *Sa-We*, 10am-9pm *Th-Fr*. Closed 1 ***Jan***, 24-26 ***Dec*** Free Toilets, bookshop, giftshop, café, rooftop restaurant.

6

Petrie Museum of Egyptian Archaeology

University College London, Malet Place, London WC1E 6BT
+44 (0)20 7679 2884 ★ www.petrie.ucl.ac.uk/index2.html

HISTORY The bequeath of a collection of Egyptian antiquities by Egyptologist Amelia Edwards led to the creation of the University College London's Department of Egyptian Archaeology and Philology, and the future Petrie Museum of Egyptian Archaeology. The museum, named for Professor William Petrie (1853-1942), now holds 80,000 items.

Despite the efforts of Petrie and other Egyptologists, there is still much to learn about ancient Egypt. For example, dating kingdoms and the Pharaonic dynasties even within decades is difficult. However, we do know that the Nile-based civilisation fluctuated between periods where Upper (south) and Lower (north) Egypt were unified, and times when they were divided. Eras when Egypt was divided are known as Predynastic and Intermediate Periods. Eras when it was unified are usually called kingdoms and commence c. 3000 BC when the king of Upper Egypt, Narmer, conquered Lower Egypt. A breakdown of eras is below:

Period	Dynasty	Start-End
Predynastic	-	5500-3000 BC
Early Dynastic	0-2	3000–2686 BC
Old Kingdom	3-6	2686-2181 BC
First Intermediate	7-11	2181-2025 BC
Middle Kingdom	11-12	2025-1700 BC
Second Intermediate	13-17	1700-1550 BC
New Kingdom	18-20	1550-1069 BC
Third Intermediate	21-25	1069-664 BC
Late	26-31	664-332 BC
Hellenistic	Ptolemaic	332-30 BC

DESCRIPTION Housed in a former stable building since the early 1950s, the museum is located on the first floor of the DMS Watson Science Library at the University College London. Up the stairs and past the admissions desk is its Main Room. Here, interspersed with other small artifacts in glass cases lettered A to H (and under them in drawers) are dozens of flint and bronze weapons. Highlights include four large, impressive socketed bronze spearheads of the New Kingdom's 19th Dynasty in Case H. One spearhead is marked with the cartouche (an oval-shaped royal symbol containing Egyptian hieroglyphs) of Ramesses II. It is contemporary with one of history's oldest recorded battles, Kadesh (1274 BC) in which Ramesses fought the Hittites. Also in the Main Room, cases WEC2 and WEC3 show a dozen bronze leaf-shaped arrowheads and knives. In case WEC9 are 11 small iron arrowheads and a very long spearhead.

Case M in the museum's Pottery Room displays a long finely woven flax sling with a thick plaited cord from the Third Intermediate Period next to its modern recreation. Nearby are half-a-dozen bronze daggers and a ceremonial bronze axe head. On the Back Stairs is a cast of the Narmer Palette discovered by Petrie in 1897. Shown in Case W, it commemorates the unification of Egypt by Narmer, and depicts him about to use a mace to smite a roped prisoner.

VISITOR INFO 🌐 1-5pm *Tu-Sa*. Closed Christmas Eve to early *Jan*, and Easter Holidays 💲 Free 🅵 Limited 🦽 Wheelchair access is via the Science Library.

St John's Gate, Church & Museum
St. John's Lane, Clerkenwell, London EC1M 4DA
+44 (0)20 7324 4070   ★   museumstjohn.org.uk

HISTORY After the Order of the Knights of St John (the Knights Hospitaller) was founded at Jerusalem in 1099, donations of property throughout Christendom financed its good works. In 1140 a donation of land at Clerkenwell just north of the City of London became the Knights' Priory in England, their headquarters in the kingdom. A ten-acre property, Clerkenwell Priory was divided into outer and inner precincts. Defence of the inner precinct was the priority as it housed the Knights' sleeping quarters, valuables, and an armoury. Formidable walls, a fortified gatehouse (the predecessor of St John's Gate), and military skills of its armed brethren were adequate protection for most of its existence.

In 1381, however, the Priory was destroyed during the Peasants Revolt. The spark for the revolt was an increase in the poll tax administered by Robert Hales, Richard II's treasurer. Hales had spent most of his career as a Knight of St John in Rhodes and made his reputation crusading against the surrounding Muslim powers. His 1371 election as the Prior of England saw Hales return to London. There he was also appointed admiral of England's western fleet.

Setbacks in the Hundred Years War (1337-1453) against France, Hales's role implementing the tax, and the Order's wealth made the Hospitallers a target of the Peasant's Revolt. When the revolt broke out, the few knights and sergeants at the Priory were overwhelmed by hundreds of armed peasants and veterans. Another target, Hales, was at the Tower of London. With him were other ministers, royalty including the young Richard II, and a few hundred soldiers. When the king went to Smithfield (near the destroyed Priory) to speak with the rebels, the soldiers inexplicably let the rebels into the Tower. They then dragged Hales, the Chancellor and Archbishop of Canterbury, and others associated with the government to Tower Hill and beheaded them.

While the revolt was rapidly crushed in the following days, it took years to rebuild the Order's properties including the Priory and its fortified gate. Once restored, monarchs passed through the gate on their way to stay at the Priory. Those monarchs included Henry IV in 1399 while awaiting his coronation, and Manuel II Palaiologos, Emperor of the Eastern Roman Empire, in 1400 appealing for Christian help against the Turks besieging his capital, Constantinople.

Following Henry VIII's dissolution of the Order in 1540, the Priory had many uses including the workplace of Samuel Johnson and the childhood home of painter William Hogarth. In the 1870s it was acquired by the recently revived Order of St. John, and gradually converted to serve as the headquarters and museum of the organization and its charitable offshoots

DESCRIPTION Areas of the old Priory described below in order of decreasing accessibility are: the gate outside, the museum, the gate inside, and the church.

St John's Gate today consists of two towers and a room joining them. Inscribed on the gate are heraldic arms including those of Henry VII and Sir Thomas Docwra, the king and prior when the gate was last rebuilt (1504).

Under the gate a glass door leads to the museum. To the right is a gallery on the Knights Hospitaller from its beginnings at Jerusalem, through sieges by Turks of its Mediterranean island strongholds Rhodes (1480, 1522) and Malta (1565), to its expulsion from Malta by Napoleon (1798). The gallery's military artifacts include helmets, plate and chainmail armor, cannonballs from Rhodes (1522), and a bronze Tudor cannon. The cannon is the sole survivor of 19 artillery pieces given by the Order's then Protector, Henry VIII, to its Grand Master in 1527. A model of a galley and a painting of a naval battle reflect the importance of the Hospitaller Navy in protecting Christian Europe from Muslim pirates.

A guided tour also takes visitors to other rooms in the museum building: the Council Chamber over the gate, the Chapter Hall, the Old Chancery, and the Prior's Dining Room. These rooms and the stairways connecting them are decorated with priors' coats of arms from Father Walter (1143) onward, and with paintings of officers of the Order and of naval battles in the Mediterranean.

Also on the guided tour is the Order's church. Located north of the gate at St John's Lane and Clerkenwell Road, it was once the innermost part of St John's Priory's inner precinct. A church was first built in the 1140s, consecrated in 1184, destroyed in 1381, rebuilt, bombed in 1941, then partially rebuilt. Its design was based on the original Church of the Holy Sepulchre in Jerusalem. Tours take visitors under the church to the Priory's oldest surviving part, the 12th century Norman crypt, to see the tomb of a 16th century Spanish knight of the Order.

VISITOR INFO 🜊 Gate: 24 hours daily (outside only). Museum: 10am-5pm *Mo-Sa* all year, 10am-5pm *Su Jul-Sep* only. 80-minute tours: 11am and 2.30am *Tu*, *Fr* and *Sa* all year. Additional tour 2pm *Su Jul-Sep* only. Call the museum for group bookings 🄳 Museum: Free. Tour: £5 donation requested 🄵 Male, female and disabled toilets are on the museum's ground floor. Gift shop. 🜞 Another crusader church in London is Temple Church. Built by the Knights Templar, the church was transferred to the Hospitallers after the dissolution of the Templars in 1312. Temple Church is at 2 King's Bench Walk, Temple, London EC4Y 7DE.

ST PAUL'S CATHEDRAL
St Paul's Churchyard, London EC4M 8AD
+44 (0)20 7236 4128 / 7246 8350   ★   stpauls.co.uk

HISTORY There has been a St Paul's Cathedral on the same site in London for over 1,400 years. The first of five St Paul's was built in 604 and destroyed by fire in 675. The second was destroyed by Vikings. The third was destroyed by fire in 962. It was rebuilt in stone the same year. After another fire in 1087, a rebuilding started which only finished in 1310. After this Old St Paul's was destroyed in the Great Fire of London (1666), the current cathedral was designed by Sir Christopher Wren and built between 1675 and 1710. Made in late Renaissance style, its imposing dome was inspired by St Peter's Basilica in Rome.

St Paul's was almost destroyed again during the Second World War when an unexploded bomb landed inside on 30 September 1940. The explosive was defused by Lieutenant Robert Davies of the Royal Engineers.

Since the first service in 1697, ceremonies of nationwide significance have been held at St Paul's. They have included funeral services of Admiral Nelson (1806), the Duke of Wellington (1852), and Sir Winston Churchill (1965).

DESCRIPTION St Paul's Cathedral – the second largest in the world after St Peter's in Rome - houses chapels, flags and regimental colours, and military caskets, sarcophagi and effigies. Carved into the Cathedral's walls, pillars and arches are dozens of friezes of battle scenes and famous British military leaders. Memorials carry inscriptions ranging from the brief "ROBERTS" (Field Marshal Frederick Roberts, Earl Roberts of Kandahar) near Nelson's tomb in the crypt through brief descriptions of careers to lengthy accounts of combat. Memorials from the French Revolutionary Wars onward can be found in the crypt and on the cathedral floor.

Dozens of memorials on the cathedral floor are to individuals (among them Wellington Memorial to the Duke of Wellington, and Major General Charles Gordon's sarcophagus) and to units (Cavalry Division of the British Army in the Crimean War; British, Indian and Ghurkha soldiers who served in the British East India Company's Indian Army to 1858 and the British Empire's Indian Army to 1947). At the peak of the cathedral's apse is the American Memorial Chapel, Britain's memorial to all British-based Americans who gave their lives during the Second World War. This area was bomb-damaged during the war.

Occupying the area directly below the cathedral's floor is the crypt, the largest in Western Europe. Two tombs dominate the crypt, those of Britain's greatest admiral and her greatest general.

Under the dome altar is Wellington's body in a simple granite casket. Around the tomb are banners made for his funeral procession in 1852, and ten memorials of Field Marshals of the British Commonwealth in the Second World War. In line of sight from Wellington's tomb at the middle of the crypt directly underneath the centre of the dome is Nelson's tomb. When Nelson was killed at the battle of Trafalgar, he had his coffin with him on board his flagship, *Victory*. Made from the mast of a French ship sunk in one of his earlier victories, Nelson's body still rests within the coffin in his tomb.

Between the tombs and widely distributed around the crypt are dozens of war memorials dedicated to the Punjab Frontier Force in Afghanistan (1878-1880), Royal Dragoons of the Boer War (1898-1902), Parachute Regiment and Airbourne Forces in 1940, Korea (1950-1953), South Atlantic Task Force (1982), and the Gulf War (1990-1991) among others. The Gallipoli (1915) memorial is marked with a metal frieze of soldiers wading ashore and map of the campaign.

Individual memorials include a wall engraving of Florence Nightingale, and Royal Air Force (RAF) pilots wings of Pilot Officer William Fiske III: "An American citizen who died that England might live" dated 18 August 1940.

A fitting conclusion to a visit to St Paul's is Sir Christopher Wren's Tomb in the crypt. His son authored the epitaph: LECTOR, SI MONUMENTUM REQUIRIS CIRCUMSPICE (Reader, if you seek his monument look around you).

VISITOR INFO 🕐 8.30am-4.30pm daily (last ticket 4pm) 💷 Adult £18, Child (6-17y) £8, Senior £16, Student £6, Family (2 adults, 2 children) £44 🚻 Toilets, audio guides, guided tours ⌖ After ascending 528 steps to St Paul's Golden Gallery 915 feet above the cathedral floor, visitors can see panoramic views of the city.

VICTORIA & ALBERT MUSEUM
Cromwell Road, South Kensington, London SW7 2RL
+44 (0)20 7942 2000   ★   www.vam.ac.uk

HISTORY This museum's predecessors were the Government School of Design (established 1837) and the Great Exhibition of 1851. Items from the School and Exhibition became part of the new Museum of Manufactures in 1852 and then of South Kensington Museum in 1857. South Kensington Museum's art collections were renamed the Victoria & Albert Museum (V&A) in 1899 to honour Queen Victoria and her late consort Prince Albert. Construction on a home for the new museum started that year and was completed in 1909. Since it opened, the V&A has showcased excellence in decorative and applied arts and design.

DESCRIPTION The V&A, notably on its ground floor (Level 1), has many examples of arms and armour through the ages and around the world as well as artistic depictions of their use. Gallery 41 "South Asia" focuses on India in the age of the Mughal Empire with paintings of battle scenes (c. 1590-1595), gauntlet sword, battle standards, tent panels, mail coat, swords and scabbards, plate armour, matchlock guns, shield, mace, and helmet (16th to 19th centuries).

One of the Empire's successors in southern India was Mysore (established 1762). A nearby display on Mysore features flintlock pistols (1796-1797), swords (17th and 18th century), and the life-sized model of a tiger that when hand-cranked would devour a model of a red-coated British soldier (c.1795).

East Asia is the focus of Gallery 44 "China" and Gallery 45 "Japan". Gallery 44 shows Jade ceremonial weapons 2000 to 1050 BC. Samurai equipment from the 14th to the 19th century - swords, hand guards, helmets, and suits of armour (Damaru, Haramaki, Yukinoshita styles) – are in Gallery 45.

Also noteworthy on Level 1 are the contents of two great sky-lit courts. Gallery 46a "Europe: Cast Courts" contains plaster casts of medieval sarcophagi of assorted knights, nobility and royalty. But dominating the court is a replica of Trajan's column: life-size, cut in half height-wise, and viewable close up. The original marble column, 98 feet (30 m) tall and 11 feet (3.7 m) in diameter, depicts the Roman Emperor Trajan's campaigns against the Dacians in modern-day Romania (AD 101-102, AD 105-106). Scenes showing 2,500 figures wind up and around the column for 625 feet (190 m). Although Trajan's Column still stands in the centre of Trajan's Forum in Rome where it was erected (AD 113), after a century and a half of industrial pollution the V&A casts (taken in 1864) are a far better representation of its ancient appearance than the original.

Gallery 46b "Europe: Cast Courts" contains reproductions of Italian Renaissance sculpture and architecture. One cast is of reliefs from the marble tomb of Gaston de Foix (1489-1512), a French military commander and nephew of Louis XII of France. The reliefs' subjects are military scenes such as the Battle of Brescia (France against Brescia and Venice in 1512), and the Battle of Ravenna (France against Spain, also 1512) in which de Foix died.

Among galleries on Level 2 is "The Civil War Years" (56e) with a royalist officer's portrait, pikeman's helmet, breastplate, sword, and sash. Also part of the exhibit are military medals (1646-1653). In the next room, "New Technical Skills" (1660-1710) has a breech-loading pistol and a flintlock gun (both c. 1690).

Various arms including firearms and armour (such as in Gallery 114c) are displayed singly or in small groups elsewhere on Level 3 and other floors.

VISITOR INFO 🏛 10am-6pm *Sa-Th*, 10am-10pm *Fr*. Closed 24-26 *Dec* 💷 Free 🅵 Full facilities 🚼 Children must be accompanied by an adult in Cast Courts.

WALLACE COLLECTION
Hertford House, Manchester Square, London W1U 3BN
+44 (0)20 7563 9500 ★ wallacecollection.org

HISTORY Numerically, the largest part of this art museum is its European and Oriental antique arms and armour, one of the finest collections the world.

Building on his father's personal collection, the 4th Marquess of Hertford bought Oriental arms and armour in Paris during the 1860s. Upon the 4th Marquess's death in 1870, his son Richard Wallace inherited the collections.

An excellent opportunity for Wallace arose from the Franco-Prussian War (1870-1871) when he managed to purchase the European arms and armour collected by Napoleon III's Director of Museums and Superintendent of Fine Arts. After buying two other collections over the next year, Wallace had an armoury of international significance.

When he moved to London in 1872, Wallace took his collections with him. He then installed the artworks in Hertford House, and on his death in 1890 gave the house and its art collections to his wife. Lady Wallace in turn bequeathed them to the nation on her death in 1897. In 1900 the house opened to the public.

DESCRIPTION Of the Collection's twenty five galleries, four are of arms and armour. All four are on the ground floor of historic Hertford House (built 1776-1788). Three galleries show European arms and armour, the remaining gallery their Oriental equivalents.

Gallery 11 "Oriental Armoury" contains a thousand items reflecting fine craftsmanship sought by collectors of Asiatic arms and armour in 1860s Paris. Highlights are Ottoman and Arab edged weapons; a spectacular sword that once belonged to the Sikh Maharaja, Ranjit Singh (1780-1839), the Lion of the Punjab; battle axes, daggers, maces, arrows, helmets, and elephant goads of 18th and 19th century Indo-Persian origin; a court dress of a military mandarin of the Chinese Ch'ing Dynasty (1821-1850) topped with a silver and copper-gilt helmet and complemented by a 27-inch-long dragon-engraved sword from same period; arms and armour from Malaya and Japan; and engraved and etched matchlock, snaphance and flintlock muskets and pistols.

The first of Wallace's three European arms and arms galleries, Gallery 10 "European Armoury I", covers the period from the 14th to the early 16th century. Among its armour is a very rare Milanese pig-faced visored helmet (bascinet) with camail (chainmail hood) protecting the neck (1390-1410), byrnies (chainmail tunics), and plate armour (plain and fluted). Weapons include bills, pole-axes, boar spears, tilting lances, and single and double-handed swords and maces.

Past ceremonial shields in a hall cabinet is Gallery 9 "European Armoury II". Most pieces in the room are from the late 15th to early 17th century. Spanning the period are two-dozen half, three-quarter and full suits of field and parade armour. Taking pride of place at the room's centre are two sets of equestrian armour for man and horse. One is a very rare complete war harness with shell-like flutings of German Gothic armour made in the Bavarian Alps (c. 1480). The other is made of blackened, etched and gilt steel at Nuremburg (c. 1535) for the Count Palatine of the Rhine, Elector Otto Heinrich (1502-1559). It was looted from the Rhineland in 1800 by the occupying troops of France's First Consul, Napoleon Bonaparte (from 1804 Emperor Napoleon I).

In contrast to the first two European galleries, projectile weapons are the mainstay of Gallery 8 "European Armoury III". Its pieces cover 350 years from the mid-16th century when firearms replaced longbows and crossbows on the battlefield. Standout arms are German wheellocks (early 1560s), Italian stone-bows (c. 1580), a heavy wheellock manufactured at Augsburg (c. 1600) that was possibly a grenade launcher, and a French double-barrelled flintlock rifle made at Versailles (c. 1805) marked with the insignia of Emperor Nicholas I of Russia. Complementing the personal firearms are small artillery pieces including a cast-bronze cannon barrel and its carriage made in Venice (1688). Armour and swords are well-represented in this gallery as they are in the other three.

VISITOR INFO ⬥ 10am-5pm daily. Closed 24-26 *Dec* ⬥ Free ⬥ Full range of facilities ⬥ Easily overlooked but not to be missed is the excellent Conservation Gallery in the basement. A handling collection allows visitors to try on replica and original armour from medieval and early modern Europe.

WESTMINSTER ABBEY AND MUSEUM
20 Dean's Yard, London SW1P 3PA
+44(0)20 7222 5152 ★ westminster-abbey.org

HISTORY Before Westminster was associated with Parliament it was associated with the Sovereign, and before it was associated with the Sovereign it was associated with the Church. The first known church at Westminster was on Thorney Island, an islet bounded by the River Thames on its east and branches of the River Tyburn on its other sides. Built c. 600 (about the same time as St Paul's in the City and the Saxon settlement along the Strand) it declined after Alfred the Great resettled his subjects within the old Roman city walls.

From the mid-10th century onward, however, its experienced a resurgence. Around 960 it was reconstituted as a Benedictine abbey and adopted as a royal church. It may have been then that it was named Westminster because its abbey (minster) was west of St Paul's.

Less than a century later, the Saxon king St Edward the Confessor (r.1042-1066) rebuilt Westminster Abbey. After his death English and British monarchs were crowned there starting in 1066 with the last Saxon king Harold II and the first Norman king William I. Henry III built the current church from 1245.

DESCRIPTION The abbey contains many burials of, and memorials to, military commanders. While kings and queens were buried in the abbey since Henry III, national leaders who were neither royalty nor nobility were allowed this honor only from 1657 starting with General at Sea Robert Blake during the Commonwealth. Blake and Parliamentarian generals Oliver Cromwell and Henry Ireton, also buried in the abbey, were exhumed in 1661 on the orders of Charles II. Captain General George Monck, instrumental in returning Charles II to the throne, still rests where he was buried inside Westminster Abbey in 1670.

Other notable military burials are of spymaster Major John André and General John Burgoyne (both famous for their roles in the American War of Independence), and – in the centre of the nave - The Unknown Warrior. Vice Admiral Sir Francis Drake, General James Wolfe, and Sir Winston Churchill are remembered in memorials. Also within the abbey is the RAF Chapel dedicated to the airmen of the Royal Air Force who died in the Battle of Britain.

Near the abbey in an 11th-century vaulted undercroft is its museum. Exhibits include a funeral helm (c. 1500), three-quarter funeral armour of George Monck, and an effigy of Nelson. Royal armor includes Edward III's shield and ceremonial sword, and Henry V's funeral helm, shield, sword and saddle.

VISITOR INFO 🐌 Abbey: 9.30am-3.30pm *Mo, Tu, Th, Fr*; 9.30am-6pm *We*; 9.30am-1.30pm *Sa*. Closed *Su* (Worship Only). Abbey Museum: 10.30am-4pm daily 💷 Adult £20, Child (6-16y) £9, Concessions £17. Family tickets available. Tickets can be bought from the Abbey's website at a discount to the above prices. 🚻 Toilets, free audio guide with admission, guided tour, shop, Cellarium Cafe and Terrace.

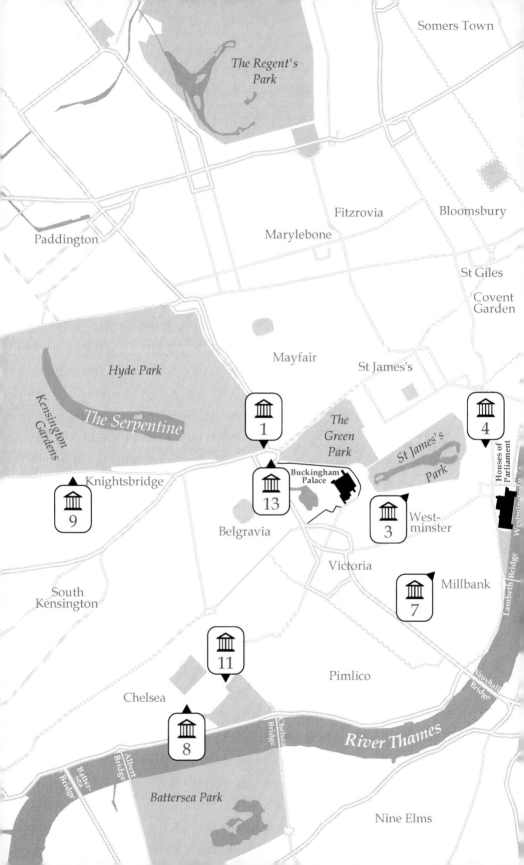

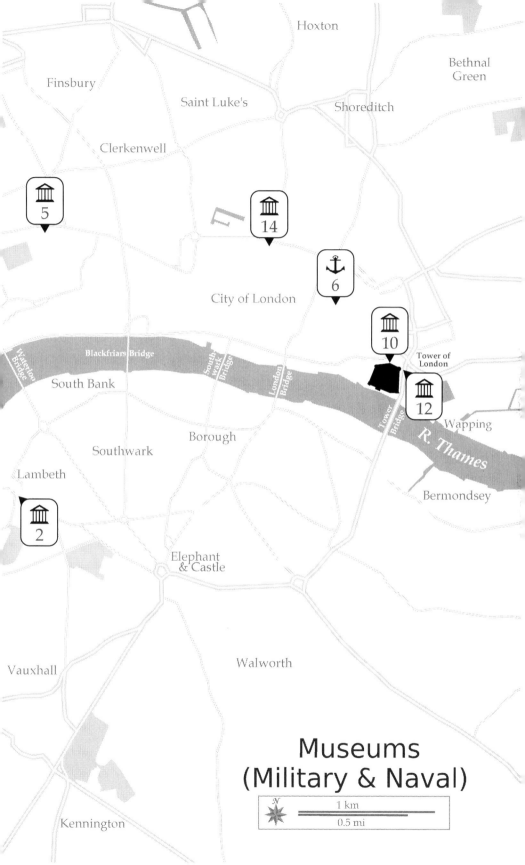

Hoxton

Bethnal
Green

Finsbury

Saint Luke's

Shoreditch

Clerkenwell

5

14

6

City of London

10

Tower of
London

Waterloo Bridge

Blackfriars Bridge

Southwark Bridge

London Bridge

12

Wapping

South Bank

Tower Bridge

R. Thames

Borough

Southwark

Bermondsey

Lambeth

2

Elephant
& Castle

Vauxhall

Walworth

Kennington

Museums
(Military & Naval)

N

1 km

0.5 mi

Museums (Military & Naval)

APSLEY HOUSE

149 Piccadilly, Hyde Park Corner, London W1J 7NT

+44 (0)20 7499 5676 ★ www.english-heritage.org.uk/visit/places/apsley-house

HISTORY British Army officer Arthur Wellesley (1769-1852) first rose to prominence after a promotion to colonel, a transfer to India, and a partnership with the Governor-General there (his brother) from 1797 to 1805. In India he conquered the Mysore Sultanate, expanding Britain's power on the subcontinent.

However, success in Europe eluded Wellesley until he assumed control of British and allied forces on the Iberian Peninsula in 1809. Five years of hard campaigning there and in France ended with Napoleon's abdication in 1814. For his achievements, Wellesley was created the Duke of Wellington that year. When Napoleon returned after a brief exile, Wellington in alliance with Prussia's Field Marshal Gebhard von Bluecher inflicted a final defeat on the French emperor at Waterloo.

From Wellington's return to Britain until his death he held senior posts in the military (Commander-in-Chief of the Army, Constable of the Tower), and politics (Prime Minister, Foreign Secretary). It was with an eye to political office that in 1817 he purchased Apsley House (built 1771-1778), a neoclassical townhouse at London's western entrance. The house appears now as Wellington left it after his renovations and extensions.

DESCRIPTION Located at the southeastern corner of Hyde Park, Apsley House is maintained in décor faithful to that of Wellington's time.

Past the admissions desk is the Plate and China Room. It displays gold-and-enamel and silver-gilt Field Marshal's Batons from the allies who fought Napoleon, as well as swords and daggers from European and Asian countries. Flanked by silver sabres and swords of Napoleonic-era regulation patterns is a unique gold-hilted court sword. Captured by a Prussian officer after Waterloo, the French emperor intended to wear the sword for his triumphal entry into

Brussels. Nearby are seven French Tricolours presented by Napoleon to French Departments and paraded before him in Paris on 2 June 1815.

Another Tricolour is in a corner of the Basement Gallery near four Eagles captured from French infantry regiments. Death masks of both Napoleon and Wellington, and a bronze cast of Wellington's hands can also be seen there. A coloured print *The Army and The Navy* shows the chance meeting of Nelson and the future Duke of Wellington in September 1805, a month before Trafalgar.

On the walls upstairs are oil paintings by Velazquez, Rubens, Brueghel, Goya, and other Masters arranged as they were by Wellington. Some works were part of the Spanish Royal Collection captured by him after the battle of Vitoria in 1813. Many decorate the 90-foot-long Waterloo Gallery. The most pervasive subjects of the magnificent art collection on this floor and the floor below are Wellington, Napoleon and other commanders of the Napoleonic Wars, and their many battles.

At Adam's Stairwell at the centre of the house is Antonio Canova's startling giant sculpture of a heroic nude Napoleon holding Nike in the palm of his hand. Made between 1802 and 1810 and then on show at the Louvre, it was bought by the government for Wellington in 1816. Apsley House is clearly a shrine not only to Wellington but also to his celebrated nemesis, Napoleon.

VISITOR INFO 🌐 *Apr-Oct* 11am-5pm *We-Su* and Bank Holidays. *Nov-Mar* 10am-4pm *Sa-Su*. Closed 24-26 *Dec*, 31 *Dec*, 1 *Jan* 💷 Adult £8.30, Child (5-15y) £5.00, Concession £7.50 ⓕ Toilets, guidebooks, children's trail, shop 🎯 Rioters smashed Apsley House's windows when the Duke of Wellington, as Prime Minister, blocked parliamentary reforms in 1830. When he installed iron shutters to protect his home, political opponents nicknamed him "The Iron Duke".

FLORENCE NIGHTINGALE MUSEUM
St Thomas' Hospital, 2 Lambeth Palace Road, London SE1 7EW
+44 (0)20 7620 0374 ★ www.florence-nightingale.co.uk

HISTORY In a few years starting with the Crimean War, Florence Nightingale (1820-1910) transformed nursing and helped reform military heath practices while becoming the most famous woman of the era after Queen Victoria.

Born in the Italian city for which she was named, Nightingale spent her formative years on her family's estates in England. In 1845 she committed herself to nursing after a divine calling. Early in the Crimean War (1854-1856), Britain's Secretary of War requested Nightingale lend her expertise to the war effort. Departing the country accompanied by 38 nurses, she arrived at the Bosphorus port of Scutari south of Constantinople on 4 November.

Initially relegated by Army doctors to sewing and washing, Nightingale and her staff were finally put to work as nurses when wounded arriving by ship from the Battle of Inkerman (1854) overwhelmed male medical resources. She continued with her staff at Scutari until mid-1856, months after the Treaty of Paris ended the war. On her return to Britain, Nightingale was acclaimed for devotion to nursing wounded soldiers and iconified in the image of her, lantern in hand, walking the wards (hence her nickname "Lady of the Lamp").

Nightingale went on to contribute to statistics research and to the 1857 Royal Commission on the Health of the Army. In 1860 she established the Nightingale Training School at St Thomas's Hospital, and also published the bestseller *Notes on Nursing*. Nightingale refused the offer to be buried at West-minster Abbey, preferring instead her family's burial site in Hampshire.

DESCRIPTION Because Florence Nightingale's fame arose as a result of her role in the Crimean War, it is undestandable almost half this museum's displays are related to military matters.

Crimea exhibits include medical equipment such as surgeons' equipment (forceps, amputation saw) and Nightingale's medicine chest (quinine for malaria and ipecacuonha wine for dysentry), and weaponry such as Russian and British muskets and bayonets, a cannon ball and bullets, and a Russian artillery officer's sword. Her notes, letters and records from Scutari's military hospitals are compl-emented by books on post-Crimea reforms of British Army health. One book is opened to a famous chart, "Diagram of the Causes of Mortality in the Army in the East", by Dr William Farr and Nightingale. Her influence on hospital design from Woolwich's Royal Herbert Military Hospital (1865) onward is also covered.

VISITOR INFO 🕐 10am-5pm daily 💷 Adult £7.50, Child under 16y £3.80, Concession £4.80, Families £13-£18 🚻 Toilets, shop, children's trail ⚔ North of the Thames is another military-related medical museum, the Red Cross Museum and Archives (redcross.org.uk/About-us/Who-we-are/Museum-and-archives).

GUARDS MUSEUM
Wellington Barracks, Birdcage Walk, London SW1E 6HQ
+44 (0)20 7414 3428   ★   theguardsmuseum.com

HISTORY The Grenadier, Coldstream, Scots, Irish and Welsh Guards are, in that order, the most senior infantry regiments of the British Army. While the latter two were raised in the early 20th century, the others were formed even before the British Army was officially established on 26 January 1661.

The most senior regiment, the Grenadier Guards, traces its lineage to both Wentworth's Regiment of Guards (raised in 1656 at Bruges, Spanish Netherlands from English expatriates loyal to the exiled Charles II), and Russell's Regiment of Guards (raised in 1660 at London on Charles II's return). In 1665 they merged to form the First Regiment of Foot Guards. After the Battle of Waterloo, the regiment was retitled the Grenadier Guards to commemorate its defeat of the Grenadiers of Napoleon's Imperial Guard.

Predating the Grenadier Guards were the Coldstream Guards and Scots Guards. The Scots Guards was formed in 1642 for use against Irish rebels as Argyll's Regiment. The unit was known as Charles II's "Lyfe Guard of Foot" in 1650 during the Third English Civil War (1649-1651). 1650 also saw the formation of Monck's Regiment of Foot, later the Coldstream Guards, for the invasion of Scotland. On 3 September, the regiments fought on opposite sides at the Battle of Dunbar. After Cromwell's victory there and at Worcester, the Scots Guards was disbanded and Monck's Regiment garrisoned Scotland.

To fill the power vacuum caused by Cromwell's death a decade later, Monck marched his regiment from Coldstream near the Scottish border to London and was instrumental in restoring Charles II to the throne. Refusing the title Second Regiment of Foot, Monck's unit became known as the Lord General's Regiment of Foot Guards, changing its name to the Coldstream Regiment of Foot Guards on his death. Although the oldest regiment in continuous service, the Coldstream Guards' service to the Crown only dates from 1661 while that of the Grenadier Guards dates from 1656, hence the latter's seniority.

The Scottish Regiment of Foot Guards was reformed in early 1662 and in 1686 transferred from the Scottish Army's establishment to that of the English. After various name changes, in 1877 it became known as the Scots Guards. While the regiment was raised the earliest, its service was broken between 1551 and 1662. Hence it is less senior than either the Grenadier or Coldstream Guards.

The Irish Guards was established in 1900 to recognise the bravery of Irish troops during the Boer War (1899-1902). The final Foot Guards regiment was the Welsh Guards, raised in 1915, so that each nation in the United Kingdom would be represented by the Foot Guards.

DESCRIPTION Entered from Birdcage Walk, this medium-sized museum is located under Wellington Barracks' parade ground.

Inside are 2,500 items from the English Civil War into the 21st century: uniforms, medals, colours, weapons, silver, historic documents as well as art, photographs and dioramas depicting the regiments in peace and war. Although the museum is named the Guards Museum, it subject is only the Foot Guards. (The Horse Guards museum is the Household Cavalry Museum - see next entry).

After an introductory video and displays, the next quarter of the museum covers the period from the Civil War to the War of American Independence (1775-1783). However, two nineteenth century wars are the ones for which the Guards are most famous: the Napoleonic and the Crimean. Extensive space is devoted to both. In the former conflict, the Guards helped thwart Napoleon's ambition to invade India by their assault landing at Aboukir Bay, Egypt, and the Battle of Alexandria (1801). From 1809 they served in the Peninsula War under the future Duke of Wellington.

During the Battle of Waterloo that finished the Napoleonic Wars, light companies of all three regiments held the north gates of Hougoumont Farm throughout battle. The farm had been identified by Wellington as a key point for breaking Napoleon's assault. With 30,000 French troops committed against it, the battle hung in the balance for eight hours. Although French troops managed to penetrate the north gates, the Foot Guards counterattacked and managed to expel them. Wellington later remarked that "The success of the Battle of Waterloo turned on the closing of the gates." Arms from the war include "Brown Bess" Tower muskets, British pistols and edged weapons (a sergeant's half pike or spontoon, and officer's swords of 1796 and 1803 patterns), and French swords taken at Waterloo.

The initial display of the Crimean War, of its first battle the Alma (1854), shows a bloodstained coatee, pouch and bearskin cap's chin-chain worn by a lieutenant in the Scots Fusilier Guards. The chin-scales broke when a bullet shattered the officer's teeth just as he shouted "Forward the Guards". A hoard of

Russian weapons from the Battle of Inkerman (1854) includes a pioneer's axe, a glass hand grenade, and a de Mutzig smoothbore percussion musket.

Opposite is a display on Guards campaigns in Egypt and the Sudan (1882-1898) marking the transition in tactics from the 17th century approach to that of the 20th century. The Battle of Tel-el-Kebir (1882) was the last time the Guards carried Colours in battle and the last time they wore red on the battlefield. A red coat worn by a colonel of the Grenadier Guards can be seen along with the first khaki uniform of a Grenadier Guards major at the Battle of Omdurman (1898). That battle was the last in which the Guards fought in line.

Final displays focus on the World Wars and conflicts since 1945.

VISITOR INFO 🕐 10am-4pm. Closed 24-26 *Dec*, 1 *Jan*, some ceremonial days, the London Marathon (mid-*Apr*). The museum advises that because it closes for private functions, visitors should call ahead. 💷 Adult £6, Concession £3, Child under 16y Free 🚫 There are stairs outside and inside the museum so access for the disabled is difficult. The Guards Toy Soldier Centre is outside. St James's Park has toilets, drinking fountains, refreshments and the restaurant Inn The Park. 🍴 The Guards Chapel is open 10am-4pm *Mo-Th*, 10am-3pm *Fr*, with the public welcome at 11am and noon services on *Su*.

HOUSEHOLD CAVALRY MUSEUM

House Guards Building, Whitehall, London SW1A 2AX
+44 (0)20 7930 3070   ★   householdcavalrymuseum.co.uk

HISTORY The Life Guards, and the Blues and Royals are, in that order, the most senior regiments of the British Army. The Life Guards traces its lineage to Charles II's exile in Flanders where two troops were raised in 1658. By the time the British Army was formed in 1661, a Parliamentarian troop - originally raised in 1659 as Monck's Life Guards - was also on the regiment's strength.

The Blues and Royals traces its lineage to a Parliamentarian Regiment of Cuirassiers that predated the Life Guards. Raised in 1650 for the invasion of Scotland, it transferred to Charles II's service in 1661 when it was retitled the Royal Regiment of Horse Guards. Its nickname "the Blues" derived from the colour of its regimental uniforms at the Restoration.

However, the Blues and Royals also traces its lineage to a troop of horse raised at Southwark in 1661 to defend Tangier in Morroco, acquired as part of the dowry of Catherine of Braganza (Charles II's wife). Upon the regiment's withdrawal from Tangier, it was renamed the Royal Regiment of Dragoons (1683) and was known variously as the Royal Dragoons and 1st Dragoons.

In 1969, the Royal Dragoons (1st Dragoons) was amalgamated with the Royal Horse Guards (The Blues) to form the Blues and Royals (Royal Horse Guards and 1st Dragoons). Although the regiment predates the Life Guards, the Blues and Royals service to the Crown only dates from 1661 while that of the Life Guards dates from 1658, hence why the Life Guards is more senior.

DESCRIPTION The Household Cavalry Museum presents the story of the Horse Guards regiments and their predecessors over three and a half centuries.

Of its three galleries, the first covers the Household Cavalry's current roles - operational and ceremonial – in uniforms, musical instrument and videos. Next the Stables Gallery allows visitors see into the actual stables of the Queen's Lifeguard, and also to try on ceremonial and camouflage uniforms.

The final and most extensive gallery is devoted to the history of the Household Cavalry from 1660 to the present. Armor, helmets, uniforms, medals, standards and guidons, swords, and firearms including a Vickers machine gun from the First World War are on show. A display on the Battle of Waterloo includes the French 105th Regiment's Eagle captured by the Royal Dragoons. Uniforms include the famous cuirasses (breast and back plates) whose use on the battlefield died out in the early 18th century. Cuirasses were reintroduced to the Household Cavalry in 1821 for the coronation of George IV.

VISITOR INFO 🌓 *Apr-Oct* 10am-6pm daily. *Nov-Mar* 10am-5pm daily. Closed on 24-26 *Dec* 💷 Adult £7, Child (5-16y) and Concession £5, Family (2 adults, 3 children) £18 🎧 20-minute or one-hour audio tours are free with admission

INNS OF COURT & CITY YEOMANRY MUSEUM
10 Stone Buildings, Lincoln's Inn, London WC2A 3TG
+44 (0)20 7405 8112   ★   iccy.org.uk/museum.html

HISTORY Inns of Court, an area immediately west of the City of London, has a long if unconventional military history. By 1189, it was owned by the crusading Knights Templar. When the order was suppressed in 1312 the area was given to the Knights Hospitaller who leased its buildings to lawyers. Previously religious hostels, the buildings became law schools and law student hostels. All barristers at English courts today must be members of one of four Inns of Court: Inner Temple (1312), Middle Temple (1320), Lincoln's Inn (1348), or Gray's Inn (1370).

Responding to the threat of Spanish invasion in the 1580s, Inns of Court lawyers, clerks and students formed military associations, disbanding when the threat had passed. This pattern would be followed down the centuries: in the English Civil War, the Jacobite Uprising of 1745, and the French Revolutionary and Napoleonic Wars. Raised once again in 1859 in response to a threatened French invasion, the Inns of Court Volunteers did not disband when the crisis passed but continued as a rifle unit. In this role, the regiment was awarded its first battle honour, "South Africa", during the Boer War. Retasked for officer training during the First World War, it changed its role to cavalry in the interwar years, then again to an armoured car regiment in the Second World War.

In 1961, the Inns of Court amalgamated with the City of London Yeomanry Regiment to form the Inns of Court and City Yeomanry. The City of London Yeomanry Regiment had been raised as cavalry in 1900, and also served in the Boer War and both World Wars.

Since 1969, the combined regiment has been tasked as a signal squadron.

DESCRIPTION Uniforms, artwork, weapons, medals and equipment of the Inns of Court Regiment, the City of London Yeomanry, and the amalgamated unit are shown in this small museum behind its drill hall on the first floor of 10 Stone Buildings. Exhibits on the left and middle of the museum deal with the Inns of

Court and its predecessors. Those on the right are to do with the Yeomanry. At the rear of the collection are exhibits from both units and the modern regiment.

Behind the panels at the museum's centre are a set of Law Association drums (1802) and a flintlock musket carried by a Law Association private in 1803. Drums and musket were most likely on parade in October 1803 during the Military Review at Hyde Park when George III gave the future regiment it nickname "The Devil's Own". In Volume 4 of his prime-ministerial biography *Life of the Right Honorable William Pitt*, Earl Stanhope wrote:

> When the "Temple Companies" had defiled before him, His Majesty asked of Erskine, who commanded them as Lieutenant-Colonel, what was the composition of that corps. "They are all lawyers, Sir," said Erskine. "What! what!" exclaimed the King, "all lawyers? all lawyers? Call them The Devil's Own – call them The Devil's Own!"

Orders and a map for just such a Review are shown nearby. Other maps exhibited were used during the Boer War and Second World War. In addition to historic weaponry (including items captured from the enemy) is a display of communications equipment: Boer War heliograph, and a Second World War wireless set installed in British tanks and armoured cars at the time.

VISITOR INFO 🕒 By appointment 💷 Free (donations appreciated) 🚻 Toilets

LLOYD'S NELSON COLLECTION
One Lime Street, London EC3M 7HA
+44 (0)20 7327 1000
lloyds.com/lloyds/about-us/history/historic-heroes-of-lloyds/lloyds-and-nelson

HISTORY Horatio Nelson joined the Royal Navy when twelve years old and rose rapidly through the ranks. He was given his first command in 1778 with HMS *Badger* (previously the US merchant vessel *Defence*). Appointed captain of 64-gun HMS *Agamemnon* in 1793, Nelson spent the first two years of the French Revolutionary Wars commanding the vessel in the Mediterranean Sea. He lost his right eye there at the Siege of Calvi (Corsica, 1794) when stone fragments kicked up by a cannon ball hit him in the face. He lost his right arm to grapeshot at the Battle of Santa Cruz off Tenerife in the Canary Islands in 1797.

It was also in 1797 that Nelson fought the first of four naval battles against France and her allies in which his role was crucial, Cape St Vincent. During the fighting off the coast of Portugal, he was responsible for capturing half the Spanish ships, even leading boarding parties onto two enemy vessels. Promoted to Rear Admiral, he next distinguished himself at the Battle of the Nile the next year. 11 of 13 French ships of the line were captured or destroyed, and Napoleon and his army were left stranded in Egypt.

Promoted to Vice Admiral, Nelson was deputy commander of the fleet sent against Denmark (1801). When the British commander signalled for him to retreat during the pivotal point in the Battle of Copenhagen, according to legend Nelson put his telescope to his blind eye, said he could not see the signal, and pressed home his attack to victory.

Nelson's final battle came four years later at Trafalgar. In 1867, Cape St Vincent, the Nile, Copenhagen and Trafalgar were commemorated in the four bronze lions installed at the base of Nelson's column at Trafalgar Square.

A lower profile memorial to the admiral is Lloyd's Nelson Collection. From at least 1688 Lloyd's Coffee House was the centre of shipping information and marine insurance. Over the next century it became more professional and moved to the Royal Exchange. In the American War of Independence, Lloyd's underwriters lost millions of pounds Sterling to insurance claims when hundreds of British merchantmen were captured by American and allied ships.

Clearly Lloyd's fortunes were closely tied to those of Britain's merchant marine, a fleet whose safety was only physically guaranteed by the Royal Navy. With this realisation, Lloyd's worked in close concert with the navy during the French Revolutionary and Napoleonic Wars. It supplied *Lloyds's List* (shipping intelligence) to the Admiralty from 1793, and set up a war charity following the Royal Navy's victory of the "Glorious First of June" in the northeast Atlantic (1794). Lloyd's then created a new fund after each battle to reward the victorious, and to comfort the wounded and the kin of the dead. Awards from charity funds are a key part of Lloyd's Nelson Collection and a symbol of Lloyd's role in supporting the nation in times of crisis.

DESCRIPTION The futuristic Lloyds building was completed in 1986 on the site of an earlier (1928) Lloyd's building. Uniquely, the new structure has its services – elevators, and pipes for ventilation, water and power – outside rather than inside the building. This leaves its core uncluttered for the gigantic Underwriting Room. Light streams into "the Room" from its barrel-vaulted glass roof through a 200-foot-high (60 m) atrium onto the Lutine Bell and Loss Books at its centre (see Notes under Visitor Info below). Alongside the bell and books is a large display case titled "Nelson: Risk Taker" containing Lloyd's Nelson Collection.

Comprised of ninety numbered items, the Collection covers Nelson's life and death. Items range from an engraving of the Parsonage House in Norfolk where he was born and raised until he joined the Royal Navy to depictions of his funeral procession and internment in the crypt of St Paul's Cathedral. In between are artworks, silver and vases, letters and other documents, jewelry and personal items, and awards and swords divided into Early Years, Battle of the Nile, Battle of Copenhagen, Private Man, Battle of Trafalgar, and Death of a Hero.

Prints (c.1801) show battle plans of the engagements at the Nile and at Copenhagen. Documents include the order of sailing for the Battle of Trafalgar signed by Nelson and issued to the captain of 74-gun HMS *Defence*.

Most important of all is 36-gun frigate HMS *Euryalus*'s logbook recording events of the battle. Enclosed in a special wooden case in front of the Trafalgar exhibits, it is open to the page where one of the ship's officers recorded Nelson's immortal signal to his fleet "England Expects that Every Man will do His Duty".

VISITOR INFO 🔱 By appointment 💷 Free ❶ No facilities 🚇 Near the Collection is the Lutine Bell salvaged in 1859 from the wreck of HMS *Lutine*. Originally the French frigate *La Lutine*, after her surrender she was commissioned into the Royal Navy but sunk in 1799 off the Dutch coast carrying gold and silver. Insured by Lloyd's, the claim was paid in full. The bell is now rung to announce important news such as the terrorist attacks on the World Trade Center in September 2001. Close by on a podium are Loss Books for the current day and for the corresponding day 100 years ago. They record ships lost at sea by Day, Location, Tons, (location) Built, and reason for the loss.

LONDON SCOTTISH REGIMENTAL MUSEUM
95 Horseferry Road London SW1P 2DX
+44 (0)20 7630 1639   ★   londonscottishregt.org/index.php?id=66

HISTORY From Saxon times well into the 18th century, England's relationship with Scotland was marked by standoffs, skirmishes, and wars. Scots referred to the English as the Auld Enemy, and to Scotland's alliance from 1295 to 1560 with England's mortal enemy, France, as the Auld Alliance.

Conflict continued after the 1603 unification of their thrones in James I of England (he was also James VI of Scotland). Even the 1707 Act of Union between the nations did not ensure peace until the Jacobite Rising of 1745 was crushed at Culloden (1746). The battle closed the door to the restoration of the House of Stuart, and opened the door to Scottish loyalty to the ruling House of Hanover.

This loyalty deepened so by century's end Scots rallied to defend Britain in the face of French invasion threats. Loyal North Britons and the Highland Armed Association of London raised volunteer forces in the capital to meet threats from Revolutionary (1793) and Napoleonic (1803) France. These forces were disbanded after each crisis passed.

Another French invasion threat, this time from the France of Napoleon III in 1859, was met by the resurrection of a volunteer force comprised of London's Scots. Unlike on previous occasions, this force - the London Scottish Rifle Volunteers – has continued as a volunteer infantry unit to the present day.

As a result of the Army's 1992 reorganisations, the company-strong London Scottish amalgamated with other company-strong Territorial Army units – the Queen's Regiment, the City of London Fusiliers, and the London Irish Rifles - to form the London Regiment. Since 2006, the regiment, in the role of infantry battalion, has been affiliated with the Foot Guards.

DESCRIPTION Two balconies around the regiment's drill hall contain its museum. Both balconies cover the period from the mid-19th to early 21st century. The upper balcony has a higher concentration of weapons while the lower balcony has a greater emphasis on uniforms and ceremonial items. Among items on the lower balcony are bagpipes, displays of ceremonial attire, and Scottish dirks (long daggers) and broadswords.

Of the dozens of weapons on the upper balcony, standouts are a Mauser 13mm anti-tank rifle (First World War), a 7.92mm MG 15 machine gun used to defend Luftwaffe bombers (Second World War), a M72 LAW one-shot 66mm anti-tank rocket (1963 onward), and rifles from the 1853 Enfield rifle-musket to the SA80 service rifle used by the British armed forces since 1985. Displays on Messines Ridge, Belgium celebrate the regiment's distinction of being the first Territorial Army unit to see action in the First World War (31 October 1914).

VISITOR INFO 🌓 By appointment 💷 Free (donations appreciated) 🚻 Toilets

NATIONAL ARMY MUSEUM
Royal Hospital Road, Chelsea, London SW3 4HT
+44 (0)20 7730 0717 ★ nam.ac.uk

HISTORY The National Army Museum was established by Royal Charter in 1960. Tasked with the collection, preservation, and exhibition of objects and records of the Army, it also encompasses reserve forces variously titled the Militia, Yeomanry, Volunteers, and Territorial Army. Non-British Land Forces in the service of the Crown are also within its scope, notably the Indian Army from its origins in the East India Company in 1746 to 1947.

After opening at the Royal Military Academy, Sandhurst in 1960, the museum moved to a new building on the grounds of the Royal Hospital, Chelsea in 1971. The site housed an infirmary (hospital) from 1809 until it was partly destroyed by bombs in 1941.

DESCRIPTION Due to reopen in 2016 after an extensive redevelopment, the museum will have five main galleries: Soldier ("lifecycle" of a soldier), Battle (how battles are fought), Society (relationship between civilians and the Army), Army (history, organization and uniforms), and Discovery (little-known aspects of the Army). At the time of writing, little is known about which of its million items will be shown. However, it is likely that its 420-square-foot diorama of the Battle of Waterloo with 75,000 model soldiers will be among them.

VISITOR INFO 🌓 Reopening in 2016. 10am-5.30pm daily. Closed 24-26 *Dec*, 1 *Jan*, Good Friday, early *May* Bank holiday 💷 Free 🚻 Full range of facilities

POLISH INSTITUTE AND SIKORSKI MUSEUM
20 Princes Gate, South Kensington, London SW7 1PT
+44 (0)20 7589 9249 ★ pism.co.uk

HISTORY Sobieski, Pulaski, Kościuszko, Piłsudski, Sikorski: a few of the best known Polish military leaders provide a window into that country's martial history. Poland was established in the 10th century, and as the Polish-Lithuanian Commonwealth in the 17th was one of Europe's largest and most powerful countries. Poland was also the pivotal player in the battle that decided the continent's fate when its king, Jan III Sobieski (1629-1696), led his army to victory on behalf of Christendom against the Turks besieging Vienna in 1683.

A century later Poles helped chart the course of another continent during the American War of Independence. Casimir Pulaski (1745–1779) and Tadeusz Kościuszko (1746–1817) were prominent in George Washington's Continental Army. Pulaski led his cavalry regiment before being mortally wounded at the Siege of Savannah (1779). Kościuszko, chief engineer at West Point and of American forces in the southern states, was brevetted as Brigadier General by the Continental Congress. He returned to Poland (1784), fought against invading Russian forces (1792), and led an unsuccessful uprising against them (1794).

Poland allied itself with Napoleon against the occupying powers of Russia, Prussia and Austria but eventually succumbed to its surrounding foes. Seizing the opportunity provided by the Communist Revolution in Russia, Poland declared independence in 1918, and under Jozef Pilsudski (1867-1935) defeated Trotsky's invading Red Army in the Polish-Soviet War (1919-1921).

Wladyslaw Sikorski (1881-1943) succeeded Pilsudski but was unable to defeat the invasion of Poland by Germany and the Soviet Union (1939). He did, however, lead a Polish government-in-exile in London and coordinated Polish forces fighting alongside the Allies. Most famously, these forces fought in the Battle of Britain (1940), Monte Cassino (1943), and Arnhem (1944). For the next four-and-a-half decades Poland was a Cold War satellite of the Soviet Union, a period that ended in 1989 with the retreat of Soviet influence.

DESCRIPTION Not wishing to return home to Communist-occupied Poland after the Second World War, many Poles stayed in London. Some of the exiles established the Sikorski Museum. Over the decades, they collected thousands of items that can still be seen today: regimental badges and uniforms, edged weapons and firearms, medals and decorations, colours and pennons, paintings and other artwork.

On the museum's ground floor, the front room features memorabilia of the museum's namesake, the back room: awards, uniforms and weapons of the Napoleonic Wars. Objects from the Second World War dominate the first floor. Its front room hosts exhibits on three topics evidencing Polish tenacity in the Second World War: the cracking of the Enigma Cipher Machine, the 1939 escape from the Baltic Sea of the Polish submarine *Orzel*, and the Battle of Monte Cassino. Among the thousands of items in the floor's back room is a fragment of a glider from Arnhem, Sten and MP 38/40 submachine guns, dozens of foreign awards granted to General Sikorski, pilots equipment from the Battle of Britain, Mauser bolt-action rifles, 20th century sabres, daggers and pistols, and Bren and Browning machine guns.

The second floor is devoted to Polish cavalry units and their successors of the Second World War, the 1st and 2nd Polish Armoured Divisions. Regimental colours, historic documents, etchings of maps and fortifications, portrait and uniform studies and landscape battle scenes by famous Polish artists decorate the walls here and throughout the museum.

VISITOR INFO 🌓 2-4pm *Tu-Fr*, 10.30am-4pm first *Sa* every month. 💷 Free 🅕 Toilets 🖊 This is London's most underrated military museum.

ROYAL ARMOURIES
Tower of London, London EC3N 4AB
+44 (0)20 3166 6660   ★   royalarmouries.org/visit-us/tower-of-london

HISTORY The Royal Armouries is Britain's oldest museum. While an Act of Parliament formed the Armouries in 1984, the museum traces its lineage to the first formal showcase armoury established at the Tower of London in 1660.

However, its earliest predecessor at the Tower dates to 1066 when the fortress was founded by William the Conqueror. Surrounded by London's hostile Saxon populace, there is little doubt the Tower then under construction needed Norman soldiers to guard it, and these soldiers needed a place to secure their weapons. After its completion, arms were stored at the White Tower, the most secure part of the fortress. Over time the Tower's armory evolved into an arsenal to supply England's navy and army.

But the Tower was not only a storage depot. From at least 1273 it hosted armour workshops of the Great Wardrobe with its own armourers. Shortly after he became king, Henry VIII established a royal armour workshop at Greenwich in 1511. Over time royal armour was brought from Greenwich and other locations for storage at the White Tower, especially in the mid-17th century when the Royal Workshop at Greenwich ceased armour production. From then, royal armour was mostly for show. While the earliest recorded visitors to the Armouries were in 1489, the paying public was only admitted after the Restoration in 1660. The Armouries then aimed to impress visitors with the power and majesty of Charles II and his forebears.

The two earliest armouries were the Line of Kings and the Spanish Armoury. The Line of Kings paraded a row of life-size models of kings of England in armour and mounted on horseback. Horses and kings' heads were carved from wood by some of the era's leading craftsmen. To promote the idea of English indomitability and the wickedness of England's enemies, the Spanish Armoury showcased weapons as well as instruments of punishment and torture allegedly taken from the Spanish Armada in 1588.

Another two armouries were created in 1696: the Small Armoury and the Artillery Room. The Small Armoury consisted of 60,000 edged weapons and firearms. The Artillery Room's original purpose was to store the artillery train but it later also stored captured guns. By the end of the 17th century these four displays - The Line of Kings, The Spanish Armoury, The Small Armoury, and The Artillery Room – were known as the Armouries, today the Royal Armouries.

DESCRIPTION The Royal Armouries greets visitors on the White Tower's first floor with wooden carvings of horses and of the heads of English kings (both from the Line of Kings), and with dozens of half, three-quarter and full suits of armour. Suits of half armour on display were once used by 16th century Knights Hospitaller, and 17th century pikemen and cavalry harquebusiers (light cavalry). Three-quarter armour was used by 17th century cuirassiers (heavy cavalry). All these suits are plain and functional, in contrast to the elaborately decorated full suits of royal armour at the floor's centre. Royal armour includes engraved and silvered field armour for man and horse (probably crafted at Greenwich in 1511 for Henry VIII), field or tournament armour (also for Henry VIII), field armour for Charles I as a man, and for Charles I and Charles II as boys. An impressive wall display consists of shafted weapons and hundreds of breast and backplates.

A film about the White Tower's history is on its second floor as is the 11th century Chapel of St John the Evangelist, and a varied collection of arms and armour. Weapons include a small breech-loading cannon c. 1500, a bronze three-barrelled breach-loading gun c. 1535, and over a dozen bills and partizans (shafted weapons), king's swords from George I (r. 1714-1727) to George VI (r.

1936-1952), Pattern swords and firearms (18th and 19th centuries), and modern firearms such as a Sterling submachine gun and a Browning Hi-Power pistol (both gold-plated). Armour here is not only of English origin (for Tudor and Stuart kings) but also from Japanese, Indian, and other foreign sources.

Much of the third floor houses exhibits on the Board of Ordnance. The Board was created in the 16th century as a development of the office of Master of Works, Engines and Guns commissioned by Henry V in 1414. Reforms in the early 1680s led to artillery and engineer trains as well as the construction and maintenance of forts being entrusted to the Board of Ordnance. The Board was the Tower's most important occupant until 1855 when it was dissolved by Parliament after uproar about supply failures during the Crimean War. Among Board of Ordnance exhibits are firearms from the 1715 flintlock Land Service musket to the Pattern 1853 Enfield percussion breech-loading rifle-musket.

Nearby are permanent exhibits on the Royal Mint and Royal Menagerie (Zoo), institutions once hosted by the Tower, and temporary exhibits such as the Battle of Agincourt on its 600-year anniversary in 2015.

Concluding the Royal Armouries inside the White Tower are items from the Small Armoury and Artillery Room in the White Tower's basement. Standout artillery pieces are bronze 13-inch mortars, the "Namur" 18.5-inch mortar, and cannon up to bronze 24-pounders field guns. Hundreds of swords, shafted weapons and flint-lock muskets with bayonets line the walls next to them.

VISITOR INFO 🌐 *Mar-Oct* 10am-5pm *Su-Mo*, 9am-5pm *Tu-Sa*. *Nov-Feb* 10am-4 *Su-Mo*, 9am-4pm *Tu-Sa*. Closed 24-26 *Dec* 💷 Free after admission to the Tower 🅕 Full range of facilities within the Tower of London 🅰 External to the White Tower are dozens more artillery pieces. Among them are 6-pounder field guns bearing Napoleon's monogram and captured at Waterloo, a bronze 24-pounder gun made in Holland (1607) for the Knights Hospitaller, a Turkish bronze cannon (1530) intended for a Turkish invasion of India and captured at Aden (1839), and a massive bronze fortress gun captured from forts guarding Canton during the Second Anglo-Chinese War (1856-1860).

Royal Hospital Museum
Royal Hospital Road, Chelsea, London SW3 4SR
+44 (0)20 7881 5203   ★   chelsea-pensioners.co.uk/visit-us

HISTORY In medieval England, monasteries were the primary providers of food and shelter for those unable to work including aged and disabled veterans. For the century and a half following Henry VIII's dissolution of the monasteries other approaches to providing for war veterans were tried. These included the 1593 Act of Parliament raising pensions from parish taxes, and Parliament's 1645 decree transferring financial responsibility for veterans to the Exchequer.

These measures proved inadequate after the Restoration of Charles II as returning Royalist forces and disbanding Parliamentarian ones meant either pensions would fall or the drain on the Exchequer would rise. Both would decrease the effectiveness of the country's new professional army because if pensions fell, more unfit veterans would remain on regimental rolls. If the drain on the Exchequer rose, less money would be available for wages and equipment.

Inspired by Louis XIV's Hopital des Invalides in Paris, Charles II found a solution for caring for at least some veterans by opening the Royal Hospital in 1692. The Royal Hospital continues its 17th century role as a retirement home for select British soldiers unfit for further duty. In accordance with Charles II's wishes, Chelsea Pensioners are organised into six companies. Each company is led by a Captain of Invalids. Captains are all retired senior British Army officers.

DESCRIPTION On the eastern side of the Royal Hospital's 66-acre (27 hectare) site is a small museum. Originally opened in the Great Hall in 1866, the museum now shares a building with the Post Office/Souvenir Shop, and offices of the Governor, Lieutenant Governor and Secretary of the Hospital. Refurbished in 2001, it contains many artifacts left by deceased Chelsea Pensioners exhibited in its three rooms: Wellington Hall, the Main Gallery, and the Medal Room.

Wellington Hall is dedicated to the memory of the Duke of Wellington. At its centre is a 1:300 scale model of the Royal Hospital Chelsea c. 1742 fitted with push-button commentary. Walls are decorated with Eagles and Colours of French Infantry Regiments captured on the Iberian Peninsula and in the West Indies during the Napoleonic Wars. Also on the wall are two halberds: weapons and badges of rank carried by infantry sergeants in the 17th and 18th centuries, and now carried by Chelsea Pensioners on ceremonial occasions. Overlooking the hall is a large painting of the Battle of Waterloo by George Jones. A key to the people in the painting is on the door leading to the next room, the Main Gallery.

The Main Gallery has mannequins in historic uniforms, edged weapons and muskets from the 18th and early 19th century. A reconstruction of a typical berth in the Hospital shows how Chelsea Pensioners live today. The gallery also presents the history of the Invalid companies and their successors, the Veteran battalions, the Hospital's responsibility from 1703 to 1863.

The final room showcases over two thousand medals bequeathed to the Royal Hospital by Chelsea Pensioners and their relatives.

VISITOR INFO 🕐 10am-4pm *Mo-Fr*. Closed bank holidays and official Royal Hospital events 💷 Free 🛍 Small shop 🎖 The Royal Hospital outside the museum contains historic artillery pieces and memorials in its grounds, and trophies in its Great Hall. Artillery pieces include a Dutch brass gun (made 1623) for the Stadtholder of the Netherlands, two guns and two howitzers captured at Waterloo, two captured in the Second Anglo-Sikh War (1848-1849) and one in the Second Anglo-Chinese War (1856-1860), and a brass gun made c. 1623 in Singora (Siam) and captured by the Burmese in 1767 and then by the British in the Third Burmese War (1885-1887). Colours in the Great Hall were captured in the late 18th and early 19th centuries from regiments of the French Monarchy, French Republic, French Empire, Spain, the Netherlands, and the United States.

The Royal Hospital Chelsea, its Great Hall and its Chapel were designed by Sir Chrisopher Wren. The public is welcome to attend Wren Chapel services at 11am *Su*. The Governor's Parade for Chelsea Pensioners is held prior to the Chapel service *Apr-Nov* 10.40am-10.55am *Su*. Note: while Wren Chapel undergoes renovation (due to complete by the second half of 2016), services will take place in the All Saints Chapel of The Margaret Thatcher Infirmary.

12

ROYAL REGIMENT OF FUSILIERS MUSEUM
Tower of London, London EC3N 4AB
+44 (0)20 3166 6912   ★   fusiliermuseumlondon.org

HISTORY Raised in 1685 at the Tower of London by the Constable of the Tower, George Legge, the "Royal Regiment of Fuzileers" incorporated two companies garrisoning the Tower at the time. To better protect the artillery train at the Tower and in the field, the regiment's soldiers were specially armed with the weapon for which it was named, the fuzil. Also known as the fusil or snaphance, this new musket reduced the risk of sparks igniting gunpowder stores.

After the Glorious Revolution, the regiment was retasked as infantry and deployed to Europe against French king Louis XIV. In 1751 it was retitled the 7th Regiment of Foot (Royal Fusiliers). The regiment's most conspicuous successes came during the Napoleonic Wars (1803-1815) when it saw action in Europe and the West Indies. On the island of Martinique (1809) the regiment captured three Eagles, each the French equivalent of a British regimental Colour.

Since then the regiment has fought across the globe as the 7th Regiment of Foot, then as the Royal Fusiliers (City of London). In 1969, it amalgamated with the Royal Northumberland Fusiliers, Royal Warwickshire Fusiliers and the Lancashire Fusiliers to form the Royal Regiment of Fusiliers.

DESCRIPTION Since it opened at the Tower in 1962, the regimental museum has been housed in the neo-Gothic building erected in 1848 as the Tower garrison's Officers Mess. To the left from the museum's entry hall is the Medal Room. Inside are all types of medals (including 12 Victoria Crosses awarded to members of the regiment), and a touch screen describing the actions for which the medals were earned.

Straight ahead from the entry hall is a fusil after which the regiment was named, and portraits of key people in its history. Next are three chronological galleries. The first focuses on the American War of Independence (1775-1783), the Napoleonic Wars (1803-1815), and the Crimean War (1854-1856).

One of the best known names from the American War of Independence is Major André. Famous for being hanged by the Americans as the spymaster of Benedict Arnold (the American general who tried to surrender West Point to Britain), André was an officer in the Fusiliers. In 1781, the year after his death, his regiment was all but wiped out at the Battle of Cowpens in South Carolina. Its King's Colours were captured in the battle and are still lodged at West Point. These and other little-known stories are covered by the gallery.

At the gallery's centre is the Napoleonic Eagle of France's 82nd Regiment captured by the regiment in 1809 during the struggle for Martinique. Near it is a Brown Bess musket, swords, and musket balls from Albuhera, Spain. Albuhera was the site of the regiment's most famous victory (15 May 1811). The Fusiliers still celebrate the battle annually. The gallery concludes with information on the Crimean War, and artifacts including a Russian trumpet and drum, and a replica India Pattern musket and Pattern 1853 Enfield rifle-musket with bayonet.

The second gallery covers the Boer War (1899-1902), the Younghusband Exhibition to Tibet (1904), the World Wars, and the Korean War (1950-1953). A wide range of weaponry on show includes a Turkish rifle captured at Gallipoli

(1915), British sniper rifle with telescopic sight, German rifle and stick grenades, and darts dropped from German aircraft (all First World War), and German 7.92mm self-loading rifle and British Lee Enfield rifle (Second World War).

The final gallery chronicles the modern regiment from its 1968 amalgamation to its deployments in Northern Ireland, Cyprus, Operation Desert Storm (1991), Bosnia and Kosovo, and Afghanistan and Iraq. Touchscreens showing the regiment's timeline and matching maps complete the museum.

VISITOR INFO 🍁 *Mar-Oct* 10am-5pm *Su-Mo*, 9am-5pm *Tu-Sa*. *Nov-Feb* 10am-4 *Su-Mo*, 9am-4pm *Tu-Sa*. Closed 24-26 *Dec* 💷 Free after admission to the Tower 🇫 Trail for children. No access for wheelchairs to this Victorian-era building. Extensive facilities are available in other parts of the Tower.

WELLINGTON ARCH
Hyde Park Corner, London W1J 7JZ
+44 (0)20 7930 2726
www.english-heritage.org.uk/visit/places/wellington-arch

HISTORY Wellington's place in history rests on two pillars: his generalship in the Peninsular War and his generalship at Waterloo. Both came late in the 22-year on/off conflict known as the French Revolutionary and Napoleonic Wars.

Looking back at the era we see Nelson and Wellington, Britain's greatest admiral and general, as equals: both buried in the crypt of St Paul's Cathedral, memorialised by monuments in central London, remembered and revered by the Royal Navy and British Army, respectively. But their sole encounter, by chance on 12 September 1805 while waiting to meet the Secretary of War, was anything but a meeting of equals. By Wellington's account, he knew very well who the already-legendary Nelson was but at first a haughty admiral had no idea of his identity. Nelson would shortly put to sea and be killed at Trafalgar cementing his place in history. Over the next four years Arthur Wellesley, the future Duke of Wellington, looked as if he would end his life as a historical footnote.

In 1809 his fortunes changed. Taking command of British, Portuguese and Spanish troops on the Iberian Peninsula, he spent five years doggedly campaigning until he pushed French forces off the peninsula and invaded the south of France. There he learnt of Napoleon's abdication and exile to Elba.

In February 1815, Napoleon escaped from exile and returned to the world stage in what would be known as "The Hundred Days". Seizing power in Paris the next month, he marched his troops into Belgium with the aim of defeating Wellington and his army before British-allied Prussian forces reached them.

On 18 June 7.5 miles south-southeast of Brussels, the forces collided with the battle raging all day. As a last resort Napoleon threw his Imperial Guard into the fray in an effort to break the British line. Their efforts were in vain. By late afternoon Prussian troops had entered the field. By nightfall Wellington and the Prussian commander von Blucher met and Napoleon's fate was sealed.

For almost a month Napoleon evaded Allied forces. But trying to escape to America he was cornered off the port of Rochefort by HMS *Bellerophon* and surrendered. Wellington returned to Britain in triumph.

Wellington Arch was constructed between 1826 and 1830 on the orders of George IV as a triumphal arch to celebrate Wellington vanquishing Napoleon.

DESCRIPTION Wellington Arch – Britain's equivalent of the Arc de Triomphe (Paris), Brandenburg Gate (Berlin), and Arch of Constantine (Rome) – is a five-story triumphal arch located at Hyde Park Corner, a traffic island and the junction of Hyde Park, Green Park and the walled Buckingham Palace Gardens.

From its observation decks, visitors can see down Constitution Road to the southeast, and Apsley House and Hyde Park to the northwest. Above its decks is Europe's largest bronze sculpture, Adrian Jones's Quadriga of the Angel of Peace descending on the Chariot of War. Dating from 1912, the Quadriga (Latin for "chariot drawn by four horses harnessed abreast") replaced a 28-foot-high equestrian statue of Wellington installed in 1846.

Inside the arch are permanent exhibits on Wellington, Waterloo and Wellington Arch as well as temporary exhibitions on related topics.

VISITOR INFO 🕐 *Apr-Sep* 10am-6pm daily, *Oct* 10am-5pm daily, *Nov-Mar* 10am-4pm daily. Closed Christmas Eve, Christmas Day, Boxing Day, Boxing Day Bank Holiday, New Year's Eve, New Year's Day. 💷 Adult £4.30, Child (5-15y) £2.60, Concession £3.90, Family £11.20 (2 adults, 3 children). Combined ticket with Apsley House is available. 📗 Small bookshop, disabled toilets ♿ At Hyde Park's northeastern corner less than a mile and a half north-northwest of Wellington Arch is another triumphal monument of the era, Marble Arch.

WORSHIPFUL COMPANY OF ARMOURERS & BRASIERS
Armourers' Hall, 81 Coleman Street, London EC2R 5BJ
+44 (0)20 7374 4000   ★   armourershall.co.uk

HISTORY The Worshipful Company of Armourers and Brasiers is descended from medieval guilds, the earliest being the Guild of St George of the Armourers.

Formed by London armourers in 1322, the guild's members controlled the production of armour in the City. They determined who could make armour and also set other regulations such as requirements for imprinting armour with makers' marks, inspections for quality, even regimens for armourers' apprentices, wages and labour conditions.

The Armourers guild had its counterpart in every craft which likewise controlled its own industry. Together the guilds governed the City of London economically and politically. As Masters of the guilds met at Guildhall to govern the City, members of each guild met at their own hall to govern their craft.

Armourers, granted a Royal Charter by Henry VI in 1453, had a hall northeast of Guildhall, just south of the future Moorgate, an area concentrated with armour workshops. They built on the site of their current hall in 1346, enlarged it in 1795, and rebuilt it completely in 1839. Both the Great Fire and the Blitz devastated the surrounding area but miraculously left their hall standing.

Just as the hall changed over the years, so did the guild. As use of armour declined, the Armourers merged with the Armour Repairers, then in 1708 with the Brass Makers so the guild was renamed Armourers and Brasiers' Company.

The Worshipful Company of Armourers & Brasiers is now one of 107 guilds, also known as livery companies, based in the City of London. Like most guilds it now has a charitable rather than a mercantile focus and maintains close ties to the military. The Armourers and Brasiers' Company is affiliated with 68 (Inns of Court and City Yeomanry) Signal Squadron.

DESCRIPTION As one would expect, the two-storey Armourers' Hall has one of the City's largest and highest quality collections of both English and foreign armour. Complemented by weapons, armour is displayed mainly on its upper floor. On either side of the staircase leading to the upper floor are two suits of three-quarter armour with closed helmets of 17th century manufacture. Decorating the walls of the expansive stairwell are a wide variety of shafted weapons and swords including rapiers arranged around a suit of three-quarter armour. Bracketing the arrangement is late Tudor and early Stuart armour for men and horses notably half-a-dozen suits of pikeman's armour.

At the northern end of the first floor is the Drawing Room and the rarest exhibits, two suits of armour facing each other across the room. One is a full suit of mid-16th century plate armour of Sir Henry Lee (1530-1610), Champion of Elizabeth I, Master of Ordnance, and Master of the Royal Armouries. The suit facing Lee's is of chainmail topped by a helmet of Islamic design. The armour and accompanying swords were trophies taken from Dervish warriors defeated at Omdurman in the Sudan (1898). A wall cabinet by the door displays a wide range of fine arms and armour. Of note are a 16th century German crossbow, a cranequin (crossbow winder, also German) from 1579, and a rapier manufactured in 1630. The other items are closed-visor helmets and gauntlets.

In the hallway and Court Room are oil paintings depicting subjects of importance to the guild. Among the art works are portraits of Master Armourers from centuries past. In each portrait, the Master's left hand rests on a skull as a reminder of his mortality.

Further along the hallway on the building's southern side is the Livery Dining Hall. Used for gatherings of the Master, officers, and 150 Liverymen (full members) and freemen (part members), the hall is the building's largest room and historically the centre of guild life. With its dome added in 1872, the heraldic arms of former Masters attached wood-panelled walls and wall arrangements of arms and armour above them, it is the Armourers' Hall's most impressive room. Alongside dozens of pieces of pikeman's armour, shafted weapons and rapiers, are the mighty two-handed swords of 16th century German mercenaries known as Landsknechts. Up to 6 feet (1.8 m) long, these swords were used to hack through the pikes of enemy phalanxes.

VISITOR INFO 🛡 By appointment 🅿 Free 🚹 Restrooms ♿ While most of London's guilds are charities, some retain a focus on their traditional craft-regulating role. For instance, the Worshipful Company of Gunmakers (incorporated by Charles I's Royal Charter in 1637) is still responsible for safe testing guns sold in the United Kingdom at its livery hall, London Proof House (48-50 Commercial Road, London E1 1LP). For reasons of safety and security, Proof House is not open to the public.

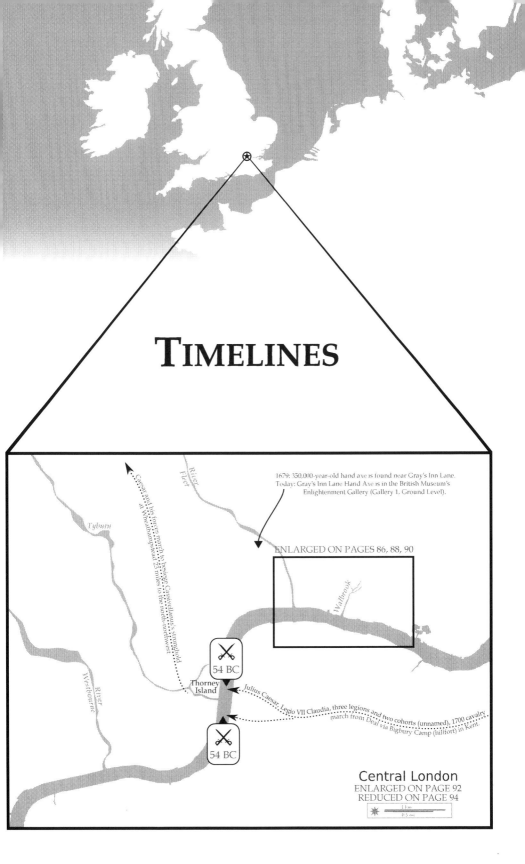

TIMELINES

1679: 350,000-year-old hand axe is found near Gray's Inn Lane.
Today: Gray's Inn Lane Hand Axe is in the British Museum's
Enlightenment Gallery (Gallery 1, Ground Level).

ENLARGED ON PAGES 86, 88, 90

River Fleet

Tyburn

Walbrook

Cassi and his forces march to besiege Cassivellaunus's stronghold at Wheathampstead 23 miles to the north-northwest

54 BC

Thorney Island

Julius Caesar, Legio VII Claudia, three legions and two cohorts (unnamed), 1700 cavalry march from Deal via Bigbury Camp (hillfort) in Kent.

River Westbourne

54 BC

Central London
ENLARGED ON PAGE 92
REDUCED ON PAGE 94

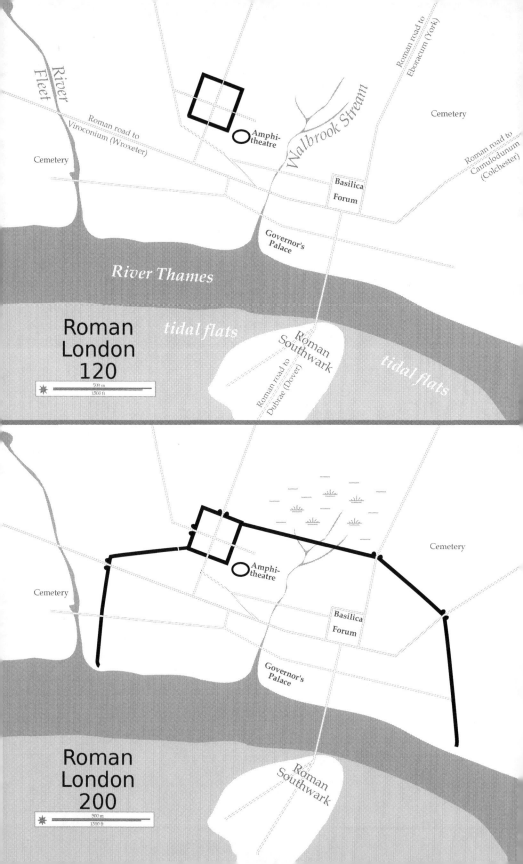

River
Fleet

Roman road to
Viroconium (Wroxeter)

Amphi-
theatre

Walbrook Stream

Roman road to
Eboracum (York)

Cemetery

Roman road to
Camulodunum
(Colchester)

Cemetery

Basilica
Forum

Governor's
Palace

River Thames

tidal flats

Roman
Southwark

tidal flats

Roman
London
120

500 m
1500 ft

Roman road to
Dubrae (Dover)

Cemetery

Amphi-
theatre

Cemetery

Basilica
Forum

Governor's
Palace

Roman
London
200

500 m
1500 ft

Roman
Southwark

Prehistory-300

From stone-age warfare ...   *... to Roman Britain under threat.*

Prehistoric dates are approximate.

To 55 BC Hand axes are used by early humans in London from at least 350,000 BC (British Museum's Gray's Inn Lane Hand Axe). Modern humans arrive from 40,000 BC. They develop weapons of stone, bronze (2,000-750 BC), and iron (from 750 BC). London's Iron Age hillforts include Caesar's Camp (Wimbledon Common) and Loughton Camp (Epping Forest). Warfare in England is as advanced as that in Gaul (France) by the time Roman general Julius Caesar first raids Britain (55 BC).

54 BC Caesar gives the first description of London during his second raid:

> Caesar [...] leads his army into the territories of Cassivellaunus to the river Thames; which river can be forded in one place only and that with difficulty. When he had arrived there, he perceives that numerous forces of the enemy were marshaled on the other bank of the river; the bank also was defended by sharp stakes fixed in front, and stakes of the same kind fixed under the water were covered by the river. These things being discovered from [some] prisoners and deserters, Caesar, sending forward the cavalry, ordered the legions to follow them immediately. But the soldiers advanced with such speed and such ardor, though they stood above the water by their heads only, that the enemy could not sustain the attack of the legions and of the horse, and quitted the banks, and committed themselves to flight.

43 Romans invade Britain prevailing at the Battle of the Medway.

47 Roman London (Londinium) is established as a commercial settlement.

60 London is destroyed by the Iceni queen Boudica and its inhabitants are massacred. Rebuilt, the city becomes the Roman provincial capital.

120 A stone fort is built in London for the governor's troops at about the time Emperor Hadrian visits the city. London's population is 45,000.

196 Britain's governor, Clodius Albinus, declares himself emperor but is defeated by Emperor Septimius Severus in *197*. Between then and Severus' death in York (*211*), London's landward city wall is built.

260 Britain is part of the breakaway Gallic Empire. Emperor Aurelian defeats the last Gallic emperor Tetricus (*274*). A breakaway Britannic Empire *286-296* is defeated by forces of Emperor Constantius Chlorus. London's riverside city wall is built to deter increasing Saxon raids.

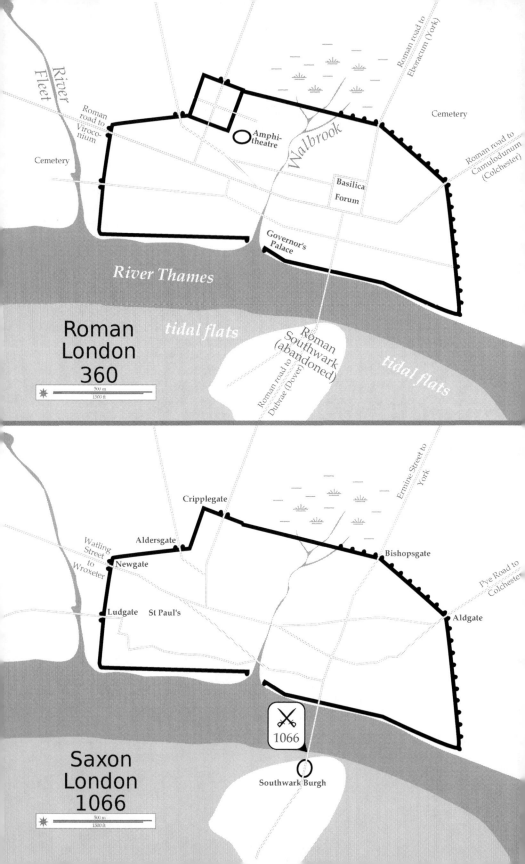

Roman London 360

River Fleet

Roman road to Viroconium

Cemetery

Cemetery

Roman road to Eboracum (York)

Amphitheatre

Walbrook

Basilica Forum

Roman road to Camulodunum (Colchester)

Governor's Palace

River Thames

tidal flats

Roman Southwark (abandoned)

Roman road to Dubrae (Dover)

tidal flats

500 m
1500 ft

Saxon London 1066

Cripplegate

Aldersgate

Watling Street to Wroxeter

Newgate

Bishopsgate

Ermine Street to York

Pye Road to Colchester

Ludgate

St Paul's

Aldgate

1066

Southwark Burgh

500 m
1500 ft

From the end of Roman Britain ... **300-1066** *... to the end of Saxon England.*

376   Gothic refugees seeking asylum from the Huns are allowed into the Roman Empire by Emperor Valens. Valens is killed near Adrianople (now western Turkey) in *378* when his army is destroyed by a combined army of Goths and Huns. Roman Empire enters a death spiral.

407   Roman Army leaves Britain to defend Italy from barbarians pouring into the Empire. Rome, the world's most populous city, is besieged three times (*408, 409, 410*) by a branch of the Goths, the final time successfully. In response to a request from Britain for help against the Saxons, Emperor Honorius tells Roman Britons they are on their own.

457   The *Anglo-Saxon Chronicle* records the last mention of Roman London:

> This year Hengest and Esc fought with the Britons on the spot that is called Crayford, and there slew four thousand men. The Britons then forsook the land of Kent, and in great consternation fled to London.

600   Saxons establish Lundenwic settlement on the Strand a mile east of Londinium. They build Westminster Abbey's earliest predecessor.

604   First post-Roman Bishop of London, Mellitus, is appointed. The earliest predecessor of St Paul's Cathedral is built in the old Roman city.

793   A raid on Lindisfarne Abbey 300 miles north-northwest of London by Norwegian Vikings commences the Viking Age. *835* Danish Vikings begin attacks on England. The *Anglo-Saxon Chronicle* records:

> *AD 842.* This year there was great slaughter in London, Canterbury, and Rochester ... *AD 851* ... [there] came three hundred and fifty ships into the mouth of the Thames; the crew of which went upon land, and stormed Canterbury and London ... *AD 872* This year went the [Viking] army to London ... and there chose their winter-quarters. ... *AD 886* ... King Alfred fortified the city of London; and the whole English nation turned to him

994   More than a century after Alfred led the Saxons into London, Danish Vikings attack the city. London is also attacked in *1009, 1013, 1016*.

1066   *Jan* After St Edward the Confessor dies in London, Harold is crowned the next day at Westminster Abbey. *Sep* Harald Hardrada of Norway invades northern England. Harold marches north to defeat him at Stamford Bridge. Harald Hardrada is killed ending the Viking Age. Duke William of Normandy invades southern England. *Oct* Harold marches south but is killed and his army defeated at Hastings. *Dec* After fighting and talks, William I is crowned at Westminster Abbey.

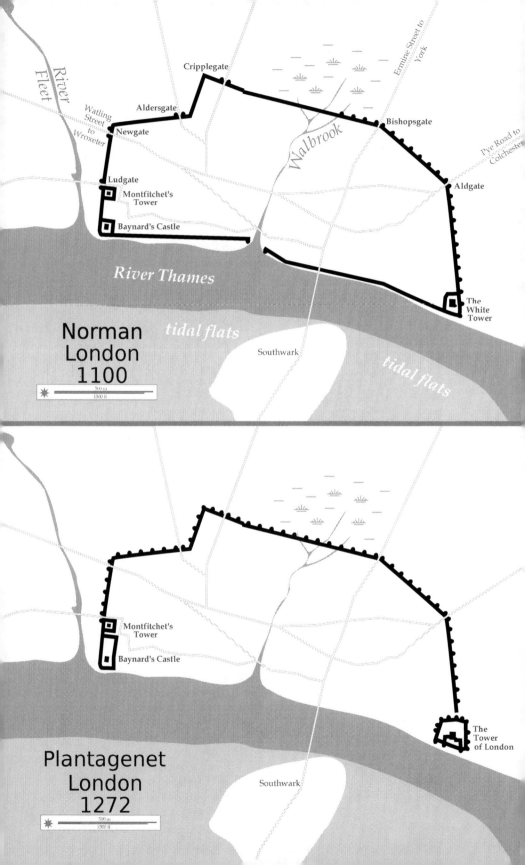

River Fleet

Cripplegate

Watling Street to Wroxeter

Aldersgate

Newgate

Walbrook

Ermine Street to York

Bishopsgate

Pye Road to Colchester

Ludgate

Montfitchet's Tower

Aldgate

Baynard's Castle

River Thames

tidal flats

Southwark

The White Tower

tidal flats

Norman London 1100

500 m
1500 ft

Montfitchet's Tower

Baynard's Castle

The Tower of London

Southwark

Plantagenet London 1272

500 m
1500 ft

1066 To pacify London's population, Normans build castles (Montfichet's Tower, Baynard Castle, the Tower of London) inside its city walls.

1078 The White Tower is completed as the keep of the Tower of London.

1141 Londoners blockade the Tower of London until its Constable changes sides from backing the Empress Matilda to supporting King Stephen.

1190 While Richard I is on the Third Crusade, his regent takes refuge in the Tower of London from Prince John, barons and Londoners.

1215 The Tower is besieged by barons and Londoners until King John grants Magna Carta and gives up Tower as a pledge he will honour it.

1216 Prince Louis (future Louis VIII of France) occupies the Tower at the invitation of barons. *1217* French retreat after defeats at Lincoln, Dover

1236 Henry III retreats to the Tower in conflict with barons. He also takes refuge there in *1238, 1263*. Henry is prolific in expanding the Tower.

1312 The Knights Templar, a military crusading order, is abolished.

1337 **Hundred Years War** *1337-1453* is fought by England against France.

1381 **Peasant's Revolt**. Knights Hospitaler properties are sacked. Richard II's ministers in the Tower are surrendered to the rebels and beheaded on Tower Hill. London's Lord Mayor mortally wounds rebel leader, Wat Tyler, then organises loyal troops to crush the rebellion.

1387 Richard II retreats to the Tower when barons clash with Earl of Oxford

1415 Moorgate built on the city wall where a postern led to the Moorfields.

1450 **Jack Cade's Rebellion**. After 5,000 rebels muster at Blackheath five miles southeast of London, Jack Cade leads them to London. They are defeated at London Bridge by Londoners. Cade flees and is killed.

1455 **War of the Roses** *1455-1487* between Yorkists and Lancastrians.

1460 Yorkists occupy London and blockade the Lancastrian-held Tower. Tower surrenders after Lancastrians are defeated at Northhampton.

1471 Lancastrians are refused entry to London. They are then defeated at Barnet 11 miles north-northwest. The Vice Admiral of the Lancastrian fleet lays siege to the City and Tower, bombarding London for several days. Unable to breach its defences, Lancastrian forces withdraw.

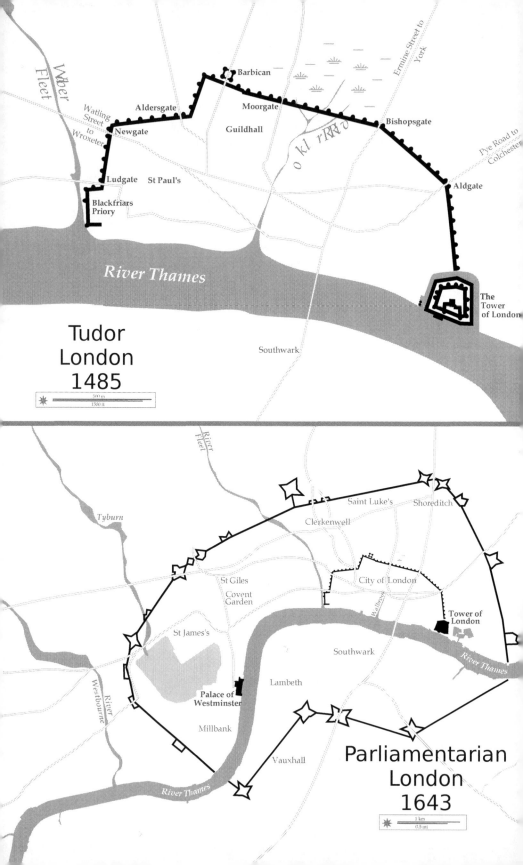

Tudor London 1485

Wher Fleet
Watling Street to Wroxeter
Barbican
Aldersgate
Moorgate
Bishopsgate
Newgate
Guildhall
Ermine Street to York
Pye Road to Colchester
Ludgate
St Paul's
Aldgate
Blackfriars Priory
River Thames
Southwark
The Tower of London

500 m
1500 ft

Parliamentarian London 1643

River Fleet
Tyburn
Saint Luke's
Shoreditch
Clerkenwell
St Giles
City of London
Covent Garden
Tower of London
St James's
Southwark
River Thames
Palace of Westminster
Lambeth
River Westbourne
Millbank
Vauxhall
River Thames

1 km
0.5 mi

From the Tudor monarchy ... **1485-1660** *... to the Commonwealth republic.*

1497 **Cornish Rebellion** Battle of Deptford Bridge three miles southeast of London between 10,000 rebels from Cornwall and 25,000 men led by Henry VII. The heads of rebel leaders are displayed on London Bridge.

1554 **Wyatt's Rebellion** Thomas Wyatt and 4,000 rebels find London Bridge guarded against them. They cross the Thames to the west and march on London. Arriving at the city wall they find Ludgate defended. Trapped at Temple Bar by troops loyal to Mary I, the rebels surrender.

1585 **Anglo-Spanish War** *1585-1604*. Defeat of the Spanish Armada *1588*.

1600 Elizabeth I issues a Royal Charter for the British East India Company.

1642 **First English Civil War** *1642-1646* Charles I and 400 soldiers try to arrest five members of the House of Commons. The members are granted refuge by the City. Charles flees London. Royalists evacuate the Tower of London. War is declared. Royalist victory at Brentford 9 miles west-southwest of the City is followed by their defeat the next day at Turnham Green. Parliament protects London (its capital) with 18 miles of earthwork ramparts and forts. *1646* After defeats, Charles surrenders to the Scots. He is placed in Parliament's custody in *1647*.

1648 **Second English Civil War** *1648-1649* Charles I secretly arranges for the Scots to invade England. The Scots and Royalists are defeated.

1649 After Pride's Purge (army coup), Rump Parliament impeaches Charles for treason. *1649* Convicted by the High Court, Charles is executed. Bishopsgate Mutiny of a New Model Army regiment in London ends with its leader executed by firing squad in front of St Paul's Cathedral. The Commonwealth of England is declared led by Oliver Cromwell. **Third English Civil War** *1649-1651* Cromwell defeats Charles II.

1652 **First Anglo-Dutch War** *1652-1654* English victory led by Robert Blake.

1653 Cromwell and 40 musketeers dissolve the Rump Parliament. They replace it with the Barebones' Parliament which in turn is dissolved before the end of the year. Cromwell becomes Lord Protector in charge of "the chief magistracy and the administration of government".

1658 Richard Cromwell becomes Lord Protector on his father's death. He resigns *1659* after recalling the Rump Parliament under army pressure.

1660 Parliamentary general George Monck arrives in London from Scotland with his regiment and reverses Pride's Purge of Parliament. The future Charles II is invited to be England's Sovereign ("the Restoration").

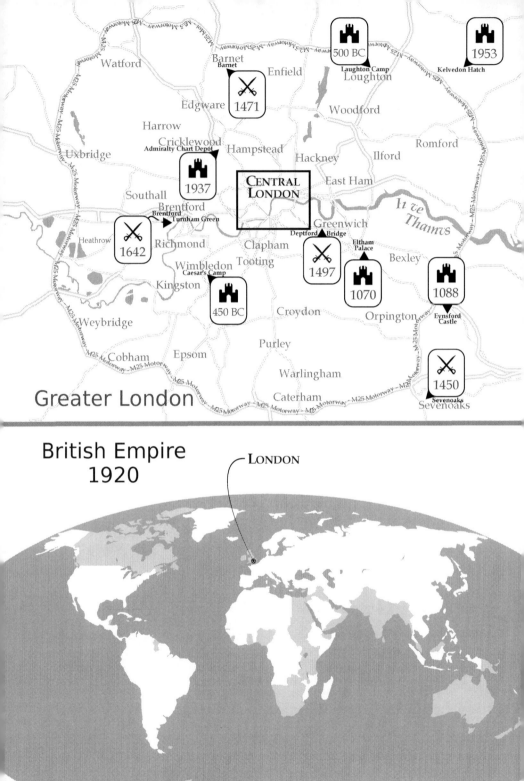

Greater London

CENTRAL
LONDON

Watford
Barnet — Barnet
Enfield
Edgware
1471
Woodford
Loughton
500 BC
Laughton Camp
1953
Kelvedon Hatch
Harrow
Cricklewood
Admiralty Chart Depot
Hampstead
Hackney
Ilford
Romford
Uxbridge
1937
East Ham
Southall
Brentford
Brentford — Turnham Green
Greenwich
Deptford Bridge
Heathrow
1642
Richmond
Clapham
Eltham Palace
Bexley
Wimbledon
Caesar's Camp
Tooting
1497
1070
1088
Kingston
450 BC
Croydon
Orpington
Eynsford Castle
Weybridge
Purley
Warlingham
1450
Cobham
Epsom
Caterham
Sevenoaks — Sevenoaks

River Thames

British Empire
1920

LONDON

From the Restoration ... **1660-Present** *... to the 21st century.*

1660   Charles arrives at London and is crowned at Westminster Abbey *1661.*

1665   **Second Anglo-Dutch War** *1665-1667* The English fleet is destroyed at Chatham Dockyard 28 miles east-southeast of London in *1667.*

1666   The Great Fire burns for four days destroying most of London.

1672   **Third Anglo-Dutch War** *1672-1674* Dutch defeat England and France.

1688   Dutch troops under William of Orange occupy London forcing James II (Charles I's son and Charles II's brother) into exile. **War of the Grand Alliance** *1689-1697* Dutch Republic & England against France.

1707   Acts of Union combine England and Scotland into Great Britain.

1756   **Seven Years War** *1756-1763* Britain gains at French empire's expense.

1761   All gates in London's city wall are destroyed to help its traffic flow.

1775   **American War of Independence** *1775-1783* US breaks from Britain.

1793   **French Revolutionary and Napoleonic Wars** *1793-1815.* On his way to the State Opening of Parliament in *1795*, George III is attacked by a revolutionary mob shouting "No king, no war." He is rescued by his Horse Guards. *1805* Trafalgar frees Britain from the threat of invasion.

1854   **Crimean War** *1854-1856* Britain and France prevail over Russia.

1859   Threat of invasion from Napoleon III's France spurs the creation of a permanent volunteer force that evolves into today's Territorial Army.

1914   **First World War** *1914-1918.* *1915* First air raid on London (Zeppelins). *1917* First raid on London by heavier-than-air aircraft (Gothas).

1939   **Second World War** *1939-1945.* *1940* Battle of Britain between RAF and Luftwaffe fighters. *1940-1941* The Blitz (Luftwaffe bombers) ravages London. *1944-1945* V-1 and V-2 rockets hit London.

1945   **Cold War** *1945-1991* Nuclear bunkers such as at Kelvedon Hatch (21 miles northeast of Westminster) aim to ensure continuity of government in the event of a nuclear attack on Britain by the Soviet Union.

2000   Attack on MI6 headquarters in London towards the end of a campaign against Britain by Irish Republican terrorists. Since *2001* they have been eclipsed by the threat of Islamic terrorists.

INDEX

More from
MUST SEE
MILITARY HISTORY

MUST SEE
MILITARY HISTORY
TRAVEL GUIDES

NEW YORK CITY

NEW YORK CITY TOP 50
REGION

CONTENTS

Center

BLOCKHOUSE NO. 1
Central Park, Manhattan NY 10000
212 310 6600
centralparknyc.org/things-to-see-and-do/attractions/blockhouse.html

Title	Must See Military History Travel Guide: New York City Region Top 50
Publisher	Must See Military History
Format	Paperback
Binding	Perfect
Size	6" x 9"
Published	March 2016
Retail price	$8.95 at amazon.com
	£6.95 at amazon.co.uk
	€7.95 at amazon.de, amazon.es, amazon.fr, amazon.it

MUST SEE
MILITARY HISTORY
TRAVEL GUIDES

Mississippi River

USA TOP 100 EAST OF THE MISSISSIPPI

CONTENTS

Title	Must See Military History Travel Guide: USA Top 100 East of the Mississippi
Publisher	Must See Military History
Format	Paperback
Binding	Perfect
Size	6" x 9"
Published	January 2016
Retail price	$12.95 at amazon.com
	£8.95 at amazon.co.uk
	€11.95 at amazon.de, amazon.es, amazon.fr, amazon.it

About

WHAT

Must See Military History is the first publisher focused solely on military history travel guides.

WHO

Must See Military History's editor, Ron Varga, is a graduate of the Australian Defence Force Academy, and holds bachelor's and master's degree from the University of New South Wales at the Academy.

HOW

In compiling travel guides for Must See Military History, Ron draws upon his life-long love of military history, his military service and studies, and his hundreds of visits to battlefields, ceremonies, fortifications and museums on five continents. Having lived in London and, more recently, in New York for almost a decade and a half, Ron has taken the opportunity to travel widely with his family in Europe and North America, and to write these guides for others with similar interests.

WHY

Military history has a lot to teach us about the brutal reality of the human condition, the struggle for survival by individuals, nations and civilizations. But it can also inspire us with knowledge of our ancestors' noble deeds, of their victories and even their defeats in the face of great odds, their valor remembered and retold across centuries and millennia. A chance to learn about and, on occasion, to visit places where our predecessors' historic struggles took place can give us a deeper connection to the past, a surer footing in the present, and strength and spirit for the future.

WHERE

Find more from Must See Military History at msmh.co.

Made in United States
Troutdale, OR
01/07/2024